Childminder's Guide to Health & Safety and Child Protection

Also available from Continuum

Childminder's Guide to Health & Safety and Child Protection

Allison Lee

continuum

Continuum International Publishing Group

The Tower Building
11 York Road
London, SE1 7NX

80 Maiden Lane, Suite 704
New York
NY 10038

www.continuumbooks.com

British Library Cataloguing-in-Publication Data
A catalogue record for this book is available from the British Library.

ISBN: 9781847060860 (paperback)

Library of Congress Cataloging-in-Publication Data
Lee, Allison.
    Childminder's guide to health & safety and child protection/Allison Lee.
        p. cm.
        Includes index.
        ISBN-13: 978-1-84706-086-0 (pbk.)
        ISBN-10: 1-84706-086-2 (pbk.)
        1. Family day care–England. 2. Children–Health and hygiene–England.
        3. Safety education–England. I. Title.

HQ778.7.G7L438 2008
613'.0432—dc22

                                        2008011632

Typeset by Newgen Imaging Systems Pvt Ltd, Chennai, India
Printed and bound in Great Britain by Cromwell Press, Wiltshire

Contents

Acknowledgements

Being a parent has taught me a lot. Spending time with my own sons has helped me enormously in my work with children and they have encouraged me to understand the simplicity of a child's innocence. Sadly not all children experience the carefree years of childhood and some experience untold suffering as the victims of accidents or abuse.

Protecting children and keeping them safe is one of the most important duties adults need to be knowledgeable about in order that *all* children can enjoy the magical childhood they deserve.

My own childhood was happy and carefree and it is not until becoming a parent myself that I have realised how difficult this is to achieve in a world full of menace and danger.

I would like to thank all the parents and children I have had the privilege of working with over the years and, in particular, those who have agreed to allow me to use photographs of their children in this book.

Thanks also go to HMSO's Licensing Division for their kind permission to reproduce core material from Ofsted publications.

My thanks go to Sam and David for teaching me how to be a parent and to Mark for helping me in this difficult role.

Introduction

Health and safety is a crucial part of good practice in early years settings and it is an issue, which all childminders should be confident dealing with. It is absolutely paramount that children are kept safe at all times.

Child protection is a very emotive topic and, although hopefully, it will not be something that you will come across in your work as a childminder, it is essential that all child care practitioners are equipped with the knowledge required to consider the possibility of abuse and that they are aware of what to do should they suspect that a child in their care is being subjected to abuse.

This book has been written to support childminders and other early years professionals working in a home-based setting. It provides the knowledge and understanding to help you to develop a positive role with the children and parents you work with and takes into account the Welfare Requirements of the Early Years Foundation Stage together with supporting the content of the Diploma in Home-based Childcare.

Further information regarding the Early Years Foundation Stage can be obtained by contacting the Department for Children, Schools and Families (DfES) at PO Box 5050, Sherwood Park, Annesley, Nottingham NG15 0DJ or by visiting their website www. teachernet.gov.uk/publications and typing Early Years Foundation Stage into the search engine.

1 Safety Within the Home

One of the most important factors which all child care practitioners must respect when setting up their business, is the safety of the children in their care. Safety is paramount and must never be overlooked when caring for children.

Children learn best when they are healthy, safe and secure, and it is the job of the childminder to ensure that their environment, toys and equipment are safe and suitable for the purpose they are intended.

Making your home safe for children

You may already think that your home is safe and that it poses no threat of danger to young children, particularly, if you are a parent caring for your own young children in the same environment. However, often dangers in the home are difficult to spot, particularly as they will change depending on the age and development of the children present. For example, if your own child is only a few months old then you will not be concerned about the dangers which may be posed by hot oven doors, as it is unlikely your baby will be in contact with them. If, however, you begin caring for a child who has just started to walk you may need to look at your childminding environment through fresh eyes, as the potential dangers to a child of this age will be vastly different to those posed for a young baby.

Although our homes are often seen as a safe haven, somewhere for us to relax and unwind, they are, in fact, a minefield of potential danger and it is not until we become parents ourselves or begin to care for other people's children that we start to understand just how

Figure 1.1 In order to ascertain where the dangers lie, get down on your hands and knees and look at your home from a child's level.
Source: Lee, A. (2008)

many potential dangers there are in the average home, all of which pose a danger to young, inquisitive children.

Children love to explore and are by nature usually curious of their surroundings. Add this inquisitiveness with their inability to grasp the concept of danger and you can easily see just how vulnerable young children are! It is your job, as a childminder, to ensure that your environment is free from any potential dangers and that the children are free to explore without risk. The only way you can successfully do this is to look in turn at each room in your home and scrutinize both the space and the contents on offer (see Figure 1.1). If you feel that a particular room poses an array of safety issues, which you feel unable to completely make safe, then you must restrict access to this room at all times when child minded children are present. The rooms you choose to use for running your childminding business from *must* be safe and free from any potential dangers.

Exercise

Before reading any further, take a notepad and pen and walk around your home looking at each room in turn. Make a list of any potential dangers you can spot which will need to be addressed. Then, after reading the rest of this chapter, carry out the same exercise again. How many other potential dangers have you uncovered?

We will start by looking carefully at each of the rooms on offer in an average home and outlining the potential dangers which you should be looking to eliminate.

The hall, stairs and landing

Children love to explore and stairs can be an attraction for toddlers who consider climbing to be one of their favourite past times! However the stairs pose a great danger to young children who can easily trip and fall. *Never* allow children to play on the stairs or climb on banisters and, when they are old enough, teach them how to go up and come down the stairs safely. Other potential dangers in this area are the following

- **Clutter** – never leave objects on the stairs or cluttering up the hall. Toys and equipment should be stored away after use and never left lying around for someone to trip over;
- **Lighting** – make sure that your hall, stairs and landing are adequately lit;
- **Furniture** – never place furniture under a window which children can climb up on to;
- **Carpets** – check for worn carpets on the stairs and in the hall and landing and replace these.

Essential safety equipment for the hall, stairs and landing

- **Safety gates** – These must conform to BS 4125 standards. It is essential that you purchase *two* gates, one for the top of the stairs and one for the bottom. If possible opt for safety gates that open rather than the ones you need to climb over as these can pose a danger, particularly at the top of a flight of stairs as the risk of tripping and falling while trying to climb over the gate is high.
- **Smoke alarms** – all homes must be fitted with smoke alarms, (the number of alarms required will be dependent on the size of your house but always fit one on the landing). Smoke alarms should be checked regularly and the batteries changed when necessary.
- **Socket covers** – fit socket covers for all electrical sockets which are accessible to young children.

The kitchen

The kitchen is probably the most dangerous room in the house and it is crucial that children are never allowed access to this room without supervision. If possible fasten a safety gate to the kitchen to prevent children from wandering in alone. Potential dangers in this room include the following:

- **Ovens** – always make sure that the oven door is shut at all times and that children are not allowed to go near them when they are in use.
- **Hobs** – make sure that any pans on the hob have their handles turned towards the back of the hob and that they are not accessible to children. Never leave tea towels or oven gloves over the oven door or trailing near the hob.
- **Tumble driers and washing machines** – make sure the doors to these appliances are kept shut at all times and, if possible, use a door catch to prevent young children from gaining access to them.

- **Fridges/freezers** – once again the doors to these appliances must be kept shut at all times and, where possible, use a door catch to prevent children from gaining access to them, particularly if you store any medication in the fridge. Take particular care if you have a chest freezer as these can be viewed as excellent hiding places for young children. Old, unused appliances, which may be stored in the cellar or garage, should also be taken into consideration when looking at safety factors. Always fit locks to prevent children from opening fridges and freezers. Young children have been known to die from suffocation after climbing inside these appliances and being unable to open them again.
- **Microwaves** – make sure that these are pushed back on the work surface and that flexes are not left trailing over the edge.
- **Kettles** – once again make sure that this appliance is placed far back on the work surface and that flexes are not left trailing.
- **Knives** – never store knives on the work surface. Always place them in a cupboard out of the reach of children.
- **Dishwashers** – make sure that these are kept closed at all times. When filling the dishwasher do this quickly and make sure that sharp objects such as cutlery are placed *point down* to prevent a child from becoming impaled on them should they trip and fall. Empty the dishwasher completely when the cycle has finished to prevent you from having to keep opening it continually to retrieve objects.
- **Toasters** – either store these in a cupboard or place them far back on the work surface making sure that flexes are not left trailing.
- **Irons** – these should be stored in a cupboard. Never carry out this domestic chore when you have young children around.
- **Plastic bags** – these can be a great danger to young children. Never let children play with plastic bags and make sure that they are stored in a cupboard out of sight.
- **Alcohol** – this should be stored in a locked cupboard.
- **Medicine** – this should be stored in a locked cupboard. If the medicine needs to be stored in the fridge then fit a lock to prevent children from gaining access to it.
- **Cleaning equipment** – these should be stored in their original containers and in a locked cupboard.

Essential safety equipment for the kitchen

- A safety gate to prevent children gaining access to the kitchen unsupervised.
- Locks for appliances such as fridges, freezers, washing machines and tumble driers.
- Consider fitting protective film to hot surfaces such as oven doors.
- A fire blanket.

The living room

Unless you are lucky enough to have a separate playroom, most childminders will use the living room as their main area for running their business. The living room will probably be the room which you spend most of your time in and it will need to be versatile in order to provide areas for play and activities as well as for relaxation. You will need to think carefully about how you can make your living room work best for you and, of course, much will depend on the size of the room and the space available. Think carefully about storage in particular. Children should be able to access toys and equipment easily without having to climb. Ideally, children should be able to 'self-select' so you will need to pay close consideration to the way you store your toys and equipment.

Although the living room will probably be your main working area it is important to remember that this is still your home and you will need to think carefully about how to best utilize the space in order to accommodate not only your customer's wishes but also your own family's needs.

Some of the potential dangers in the living room which you will need to address include the following:

- **Floor space** – make sure that this is as clutter free as possible. Obviously, young children will need to have toys out to play; however, try to get into the habit of encouraging children to put something away before allowing them to get another toy out. Not only will this reduce the risk of tripping and falling if the floor space is covered with toys, it will also make it much easier to find toys at a later date if they are stored away sensibly rather than all thrown into a huge toy box at the end of the day. Putting toys and equipment away carefully and thoughtfully will also reduce the number of breakages.
- **Toys** – make sure that you check toys regularly in order to reduce the risk of danger to children. Broken toys and toys with missing pieces can pose a hazard to young children. When tidying toys away, get into the habit of giving them a quick check to make sure that they are not broken and then spend some time at the end of each week checking all your toys thoroughly. If a toy can not be mended then throw it away immediately. If it can be mended put it to one side, out of the reach of the children, until you have the time to get it fixed. Never put a broken toy back into the toy box.
- **Ornaments** – apart from the obvious risk of breakages, you would be wise to keep your ornaments to a minimum in the rooms where you will be carrying out your childminding duties as small objects can pose a risk to young children.
- **Storage** – as I mentioned earlier you will need to think long and hard about the type of storage you will need for your living room. It will need to be unobtrusive but functional if you are intending to store most of your toys in your living room. The other option, of course, is to store toys in boxes in another room and bring these into the living room when you are childminding, but this may mean carting a lot of heavy boxes around regularly and, of course, the children will be limited to what they are allowed to play with. If you opt for shelves make sure that these are securely fastened to the wall and that children do not have to climb to reach anything.
- **Plants** – ideally your childminding areas will be void of any plants. Some house plants can be poisonous if eaten and are best avoided completely.
- **Fires** – if you have a working fire it is essential that you fit a fireguard around the *whole* of the fire place at all times while you are carrying out your childminding duties. Remember that in addition to burns, fires pose a threat if objects are placed in or too close to them, and children should never be left alone in a room where the fire is switched on, even with the use of a correctly fitted fireguard.

- **Hot drinks** – never place cups of tea or coffee on tables which can be reached by children. Many scalds to young children are the result of them having pulled a hot drink onto themselves and the burns from these beverages can scar a child for life.
- **Cigarettes** – it is illegal for *anyone* to smoke on the premises while you are carrying out your childminding duties. If you are a smoker then you must ensure that all cigarettes, matches and lighters are kept out of the sight and reach of children at all times.
- **Televisions, videos, DVD recorders etc.** – flexes from electrical appliances can pose a danger if children or adults were to trip over them. Make sure that no flexes are left trailing and never over-load sockets as this can pose a risk from fire. Use guards to protect video and DVD recorders.

One of the best ways to ensure that your home is safe for children is to look at things *through their eyes*. Adults are much taller than children and will, therefore, often miss many of the potential dangers which pose a threat to young children. Drop to your knees and crawl around your home! Do you see anything different from this level? Are the edges of the coffee table, positioned in the middle of the room, on level with your eyes? If so consider fixing corner covers or, better still, position the coffee table somewhere else while you are caring for children. What about the lidded toy box, great for storage but placed underneath the window: could this be seen as an ideal climbing frame for children to reach the window sill?

It is difficult to balance making your premises safe with retaining your 'home' environment; however, it is vital that you get this balance right. No one is expecting you to turn your home into a padded cell and, after all, most parents will choose a childminder because they prefer the 'home from home' environment to the purpose built nursery premises on offer, but this is no excuse for being lax with safety measures. It is important that you view safety as an ongoing commitment, something which will need to be reviewed and changed periodically as and when the children in your care progress in their stages of development.

Essential safety equipment for the living room

- Fireguard – this must be large enough to fit around the *whole* of the fire and fireplace and it must be securely fastened to the wall.
- Covers for video and DVD recorders will prevent children from placing fingers or objects inside.
- Socket covers for electrical sockets which are accessible to children.
- Corner covers for coffee tables or other furniture with sharp corners.

The playroom

If you are lucky enough to have a playroom from which to run your childminding business, you will effectively have a 'blank canvas' to work from and will be able to take all the safety considerations into account without having the added problem of addressing your family's needs for a comfortable home environment.

Once again a lot will depend on the size of the room but, if possible, try to allow certain areas for activities such as a quiet corner for reading and resting, an activity area with a table for painting, drawing, doing jigsaws etc. and a large space for children to play using building bricks, farm animals, vehicles etc. Over time, when finances allow, you may like to add a dressing up area or sand tray. Having access to a playroom, from which to run your childminding business, opens up all sorts of possibilities which, with a little imagination, can be endless.

Safety issues, however, are still paramount although, hopefully, in a playroom intended for children, these should be much easier to address. The everyday safety issues associated with running a childminding business from your living areas such as storage problems, ornaments, plants etc. shouldn't be an issue in a playroom.

Essential safety equipment for the playroom

- **Socket covers** for any electrical sockets which are accessible to children. If you are designing your playroom from scratch consider having these positioned high so that they are out of the reach of young children, thus, eliminating the need for covers.
- **Fireguard** – if your playroom is fitted with a fireplace it is essential that you fit a guard to cover the whole of the fireplace and its surround and this must be securely fastened to the wall.

The dining room

Although, usually, this room will only be used for eating, some childminders, who do not have access to a playroom, use the dining room as an extension of their living space and allow children to sit at the table to draw, paint, use play dough etc. and once again safety issues must be addressed.

One of the main ways to ensure that children are safe when eating and drinking is to encourage them to sit at the table. Children should never be allowed to wander around when consuming food or drink nor should they be left unattended.

Some of the potential dangers in the dining room, which you will need to address, include the following:

- **Tables** – never place objects near the edge of a table which can be reached by young children.
- **Table cloths** – when using table cloths make sure that they do not hang over the edge of the table making it possible for children to tug on them and pull objects from the table down on top of themselves.
- **Seating** – you must provide adequate seating so that all the children can sit at the table together and in comfort. Seating may consist of high chairs or booster seats, depending on the age of the children you are caring for, and you will also need to provide safety harnesses. Never use chairs which 'clamp' onto the edge of a table as these can be unstable and cause the table to tip over.
- **Crockery** – depending on the age of the children you are caring for, you may prefer to provide plastic or melamine crockery to avoid breakages and the dangers these pose.

- **Cutlery** – always make sure that children are provided with cutlery which is appropriate for their age. Young children should be given child-sized cutlery. Teach children how to use cutlery correctly, for example, discourage them from playing with knives and forks or putting knives into their mouths.

Always make sure that you supervise children whenever they are eating and drinking and *never* prop a baby up with a feeding bottle.

Essential safety equipment for the dining room

- Socket covers for any electrical sockets which are accessible to children.
- If your dining room has a fireplace make sure that it is fitted with a fireguard which covers the whole of the fireplace.

The bedrooms or sleeping areas

Children should be in your sight or within your hearing at all times when you are childminding, and this includes when they are taking a nap. You will need to think carefully about which area of your house you are going to use for children to sleep in if your bedrooms are not within earshot of the usual rooms in which you will be childminding. Some childminders use an area of the playroom or living room for children to take their afternoon nap. What ever you decide, it is essential that you address any potential dangers such as the following:

- **Beds/cots** – always make sure that any beds or cots you purchase conform to legal standards. Mattresses should fit snugly and meet British safety standards. If you are using a cot resist purchasing the type, which has sides which slide down unless they have child-friendly, secure fastenings. Never place a young child in a top bunk. If you choose to use a side rail for beds remember that, although these are designed to prevent young children from falling out of bed, they are also often seen as potential climbing frames and the hazards posed in this instance can be just as dangerous. Never situate beds or cots underneath a window.
- **Bedding** – children should be provided with their own clean bed linen. Do not use duvets for young children.
- **Pillows** – never use pillows for children under the age of 18 months.
- **Blinds** – make sure that there are no trailing cords from blinds or other window dressings which a child can become entangled in.
- **Cot mobiles** – once a baby is able to pull themselves up or stand unaided you should remove cot mobiles. Mobiles can however be fastened securely to the ceiling to prevent any risk of danger.

Essential safety equipment for sleeping areas

- Socket covers for any electrical sockets accessible to children.

The bathroom and toilet

The bathroom and toilet can pose numerous potential dangers to young children and, as in other rooms, supervision is paramount. However, you must take care to respect the privacy of older children and you will need to adapt the amount of supervision you give each child as they get older, in order to take their privacy into account.

Some of the potential dangers present in the bathroom and toilet include the following:

- **Medicines and toiletries** – these should be kept in a locked cabinet out of reach of children.
- **Cleaning materials and air fresheners** – *never* leave these out in the bathroom. Make sure they are kept out of the reach of children and never leave toilet cleaners next to the toilet.
- **Floors** – often water which has been splashed on to the floor will result in the surface being slippery. Always wipe and dry any wet floors immediately.
- **Water** – never allow the temperature of your hot water to exceed 54°C. When filling a bath or sink for washing, always turn on the cold water tap first and make sure that you test the water first before allowing a child to use it.
- **Toilet** – young children should never be expected to climb to reach the toilet. If you are caring for young children who are no longer in nappies and have passed the stage of using a potty it is essential that you provide a step for them to reach the toilet and, if necessary, a child's seat to fit over the adult seat for their comfort.

Essential safety equipment for bathrooms

- A lockable cabinet for storing medicines and toiletries.
- A non-slip bath mat.
- A bath thermometer.
- A step for young children to reach the toilet safely without having to climb.
- A child's toilet seat which fits snugly over the adult seat.

It is not always easy to spot the potential dangers in your home and, as these dangers will change when children become more active and mobile, it is often useful to refer to a checklist to help you to determine which areas of your home are hazardous to young children. By looking carefully, and really scrutinizing each room in your house, you will be able to eliminate as many potential risks as possible. Use the following Risk Assessment Checklists to identify any potential problems in your setting.

Hall, stairs and landing: Risk assessment checklist

List of risks to be aware of:

- Dangerous items such as cigarettes, matches, plastic bags, medication.
- Uncovered electrical sockets.

- Low-level glass such as windows and doors.
- Portable heaters.
- Houseplants which could be poisonous.
- Rugs which could be tripped over.
- Loose or frayed carpets on the stairs.
- Hot radiators.
- Windows without catches.
- Smoke alarms which are either not fitted or not working.
- Banisters or railings which are not secure and which wobble when touched.
- Banisters or railings with spaces where children could trap their heads or hands.
- Blocked fire exits.
- Clutter on the stairs.
- Stair gates not fitted.

What risks have been identified?	What action has been taken?	Date

Kitchen: Risk assessment checklist

List of risks to be aware of:

- Dangerous items such as cigarettes, matches, plastic bags, medication.
- Uncovered electrical sockets.
- Dangerous items such as knives, cleaning fluids etc. being accessible to children.
- Flexes trailing from kettles, microwaves, irons etc.
- Lack of fire blanket or fire extinguisher.
- Unhygienic food preparation or storage arrangements.
- Pets allowed near food, tables or work surfaces.
- Lack of hygienic dish cloths, tea towels etc.
- Access of children to pet bowls, litter trays etc.
- Oven door hot.
- Fridges, washing machines, tumble driers etc. not fitted with locks.
- Smoke alarms which are either not fitted or not working.
- Dustbins without lids.

What risks have been identified?	What action has been taken?	Date

Living room/playroom: Risk assessment checklist

List of risks to be aware of:

- Fires left unguarded.
- Dangerous items such as cigarettes, matches, alcohol or medication left within reach of children.
- Houseplants which could be poisonous.
- Rugs which could be tripped over.
- Loose or frayed carpets.
- Hot radiators.
- Windows without catches.
- Broken or dirty toys.
- Toys which do not conform to safety standards.
- Smoke alarms which are either not fitted or not working properly.
- Low-level glass in windows, doors or coffee tables.
- Unprotected corners on low-level coffee tables or other furniture.
- Dangerous storage facilities for toys and equipment.
- Shelving units not fastened to the wall.
- Blocked fire exits.
- Trailing flexes on electrical equipment such as televisions, lamps, etc.

What risks have been identified?	What action has been taken?	Date

Dining room: Risk assessment checklist

List of risks to be aware of:

- Fires left unguarded.
- Dangerous items such as cigarettes, matches, alcohol or medication left within reach of children.
- Houseplants which could be poisonous.
- Rugs which could be tripped over.
- Loose or frayed carpets.
- Hot radiators.

- Windows without catches.
- Equipment which does not conform to safety standards.
- Table cloths left trailing over the edge of the table.
- Smoke alarms which are either not fitted or not working properly.
- Low-level glass in windows, doors or coffee tables.
- Inadequate seating.
- Highchairs without harnesses.
- Blocked fire exits.
- Inadequate age-appropriate crockery/cutlery.

What risks have been identified?	What action has been taken?	Date

Bedroom/sleeping areas: Risk assessment checklist

List of risks to be aware of:

- Dangerous items such as cigarettes, matches, alcohol or medication left in reach of children.
- Houseplants which could be poisonous.
- Rugs which could be tripped over.
- Loose or frayed carpets.
- Hot radiators.
- Windows without catches.
- Equipment which does not conform to safety standards.
- Smoke alarms which are either not fitted or not working.
- Low-level glass in windows, doors.
- Blind pulls or curtain cords which are left dangling.
- Blocked fire exits.
- Furniture which is positioned under windows.

What risks have been identified?	What action has been taken?	Date

---

Bathroom and toilet: Risk assessment checklist

List of risks to be aware of:

- Dangerous items such as medication, toiletries, razor blades etc. left within reach of children
- Electrical switches – these should be pull cords.
- Rugs which could be tripped over.
- Wet floors.
- Hot radiators.
- Slippery baths and shower trays.
- Unhygienic flannels, towels or nappy changing arrangements.
- Water which is too hot.

What risks have been identified?	What action has been taken?	Date

---

Choosing equipment

There is a great deal of nursery equipment on the market today and choosing which type of equipment to purchase can be quite difficult. Childminders need to choose equipment which is safe, practical and durable (see Figure 1.2). Although cost may at times be an issue, it is important to remember that a child's safety must *never* be compromised to save a few pounds. Always purchase the best quality you can afford and never buy anything which does not conform to British Standards.

You should be extra vigilant when making purchases from jumble sales and car boot sales and, if possible, buy all your equipment from a reputable retailer.

Figure 1.2 Always check toys and equipment carry one of the safety standards logos.
Source: Lee, A. (2008)

As a childminder you have a professional responsibility towards the children in your care and their parents to choose equipment, including all toys, furniture, fittings and materials that will be used with or by the children, which is safe and appropriate to the age and stages of development of the children they are intended for.

Despite a European Directive being introduced into British law by the Toys Safety Regulations 1995 as part of the Consumer Protection Act 2002 it is still possible for illegal and unsafe toys to be purchased in this country. It is always good practice to look for one of the safety symbols or logos associated with safety approval in this country such as the lion mark (the logo of the British Toy and Hobby Association), or the EC symbol (the European Community symbol which means the toy meets European standards).

Nannies

If you are using toys and equipment in the child's own home it is good practice to discuss toy and equipment safety with the child's parents and to decide together which items are suitable. It is important that you are in agreement with the parents about what to do regarding toys or equipment which you are not happy to use or that you feel uncomfortable allowing the children access to. *Never* compromise a child's safety in order to appease a parent!

The following gives an idea of the safety issues you should be concerned with regarding the main items of equipment and toys and will help you to identify what to look out for in terms of safety:

- **Highchairs** – This piece of equipment must be fitted with an adjustable safety harness which fastens securely and comfortably. The highchair must have legs which are level and must be placed on a flat floor so that it does not wobble. Never leave a child unattended in a high chair.
- **Table-mounted chairs** – These items of equipment are very unstable and should not be used by childminders or nannies.
- **Baby seats** – This piece of equipment must be fitted with an adjustable safety harness which fastens securely and comfortably. Never place a baby seat with the child strapped inside on the top of a table or work surface. Check the baby seat for loose fabric or worn or broken parts. Never purchase a car baby seat second hand and, if you are in any doubt about how the seat should be fitted in the car, seek professional advice. Never leave a child unattended in a car seat.
- **Baby walkers** – This piece of equipment is potentially very dangerous as it can easily overbalance and tip the child out. Home-based child carers are not advised to use this type of equipment.
- **Cots** – Remember that children can climb out of cots. Cots should be kept for sleeping in and should not be used for playing. If you have a cot which has sides that slide down, make sure that these have secure fastenings which are child proof. Mattresses should conform to safety standards and fit snugly around the frame.
- **Beds** – Childminders should never place a young child in a top bunk. If you opt for bed guards be wary as young children can see these as climbing frames. Mattresses should conform to safety standards and fit snugly around the frame.

- **Pillows** – Children under the age of 18 months should not be given a pillow.
- **Safety gates** – should conform to safety standards and be placed at both the top and bottom of the stairs and to prevent access to rooms which pose a danger, such as the kitchen. Opt for gates which open rather than the cheaper versions which have to be climbed over.
- **Prams and buggies** – check for broken or missing parts and repair or replace immediately. Always use a secure, adjustable harness to fasten babies and children into buggies and prams.
- **Toilet seats/Steps** – check for cracks or splits in the plastic and replace when necessary. Children should never be expected to climb to reach a toilet and a suitable non-slip step should be provided.

Using equipment safely

Keeping children safe is not just a matter of purchasing equipment which conforms to the necessary standards. The way we use toys and equipment and the way in which we teach children to use them are all part of keeping safe.

One of the most important factors, which everyone can contribute to, is to keep things tidy. Tidying up regularly has several advantages:

- It keeps the floor clutter free, therefore, reducing the risk of tripping and falling over objects left out.
- It keeps toys and equipment in a good state of repair – putting things away periodically will prevent them getting broken if they are stood on.
- It prevents parts becoming lost – tidying a jigsaw away as soon as it is finished with, for example, will reduce the risk of any pieces getting lost or mixed up with other toys.

Many accidents are caused, not just by faulty toys and equipment, but also by carelessness and the desire to either play with items which are unsuitable, or by failing to realize the threat of danger from using toys and equipment inappropriately. As a childminder you have a duty to ensure that the children in your care understand the importance of using toys and equipment in the nature for which they were designed and by setting a good example yourself, you will be encouraging children to act sensibly and stay safe.

Exercise

Read the following statements and decide why they are unsafe. How would you explain to children that what they are doing can compromise their safety? What should you encourage the child to do instead?

- Two 5-year-old boys are jumping up and down on your sofa, using it as a trampoline.
- A 2-year-old is walking around the house drinking from a cup.
- An 18-month-old child is building with lego.
- A 4-year-old is playing on the stairs.

Maintaining equipment

It is vital that you check your toys and equipment regularly for signs of breakages and wear and tear. Any toy and equipment with broken or missing parts should either be repaired or replaced immediately.

It is good practice to check toys everyday when tidying them away and to do a thorough check at the end of each week. This may sound very time consuming, particularly if you have a large selection of toys; however, if you get into the habit of putting things away methodically it will reduce the amount of time needed for checking (see Figure 1.3). For example, store all your baby toys in a separate box from toddler items and use separate boxes for items such as jigsaws and games, animals and vehicles. This will make it easier for you to find toys

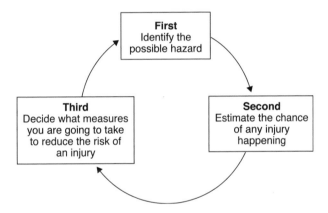

Figure 1.3 Risk assessment process.
Source: Lee, A. (2007b)

Table 1.1 Safety checklist for toys

Toy checked	Date	Action taken to make safe
Dolls house	01/07/07	No action needed – good condition
Box of vehicles	01/07/07	Three cars were thrown away due to missing or broken parts. Replaced these cars on 06/07/07
Dressing up clothes	01/07/07	Torn cape, broken wand. Cape was mended. Wand was thrown away and a replacement bought 06/07/07

Source: Lee, A. (2008)

Table 1.2 Safety checklist for equipment

Equipment checked	Date	Action taken to make safe
Highchair	04/07/07	Safety harness starting to fray – replaced on 05/07/07
Pushchair	04/07/07	Pushchair and harness in good condition no action needed
Safety gate	04/07/07	Working loose from wall, bolts need tightening up – done immediately

Source: Lee, A. (2008)

appropriate to the age and stage of development of the children you have present and will enable you to check the toys for safety.

It is a good idea to make a safety checklist for your toys and equipment (see Table 1.1 and 1.2), which you can refer to, to enable you to be certain which toys and equipment have been checked and when. You can also make a note of your findings and any action taken.

It is good practice for childminders to have a health and safety policy in place for their setting, which they should share with parents. Explain why you have your policy and discuss the points listed so that *everyone* is aware of the need for practicing good health and safety procedures. A copy of the policy should be given to the parents and one displayed on the wall of the setting or placed in your information file, to be referred to as and when necessary.

A health and safety policy should be individual to each childminder and their setting but may look something like the following:

Health and Safety Policy

I will ensure that I comply with the following procedures at all times while conducting my childminding duties:

1 I will hold a valid First Aid Certificate, and update my training as and when necessary.

2 I will ensure that all my indoor and outdoor areas, toys and equipment are safe and free from hazards at all times.

3 I will devise and follow an emergency procedure plan and practice a fire drill with the children regularly.

4 I will keep accurate, up-to-date records of all contact numbers for parents/carers.

5 I will ensure that only prescribed medication is administered, when requested by the parents in writing.

6 I will ensure that all illnesses and accidents are recorded accurately.

7 I will ensure that all dangerous substances such as medicines are kept out of the reach of children at all times.

8 I will ensure that I have written permission from parents/carers prior to any planned outings.

9 I will ensure that smoke alarms and fire blankets are in place and in good working order.

10 I will ensure that children are encouraged to practice high standards of personal hygiene.

11 I will ensure that no one smokes on the premises while I am carrying out my childminding duties.

12 I will ensure that child protection policies and guidelines are in place and followed at all times.

13 I will ensure that safe, hygienic methods are practised in relation to the storing, preparing and cooking of food and snacks and the disposal of any waste products at all times.

14 I will ensure that my first aid box is fully stocked and that the contents are regularly checked and replenished when necessary.

YOU HAVE MY UTMOST ASSURANCE THAT THE HEALTH AND SAFETY OF THE CHILDREN IN MY CARE IS PARAMOUNT AT ALL TIMES.

Exercise

• Write a 'Health and Safety Policy' which you could use for your own childminding setting.

2 Health and Hygiene

Making your home healthy

As a childminder your home will be open to scrutiny everyday from the parents of the children you care for. From time to time you may be visited by Ofsted or other professionals related to your field of work. It is because of this scrutiny that you need to be completely sure that your home is a healthy place for children to be in and that your own personal hygiene standards are high. For you to ensure that children are kept safe and free from harm you will need to be certain that you provide a hygienic environment and that all the procedures and practices you follow prevent the spread of infection.

It is not sufficient to simply spring clean your home from time to time, run around with a vacuum cleaner or dust the surfaces every few days. You will need to thoroughly clean your home regularly and pay special attention to areas such as the toilet, which will probably be used everyday by numerous people.

Hand washing

Hand washing is probably one of the simplest most effective ways of preventing the spread of infection *provided* it is done correctly. Holding hands under running water for a few seconds does *not* constitute washing them and children need to be taught the importance of this routine procedure. Set good examples for the children at all times and let them see you wash your hands frequently and correctly.

Hands should be washed

- after visiting the toilet
- before and after dealing with cuts and grazes
- after coughing and sneezing
- after blowing noses
- after changing nappies
- after wiping bottoms
- before preparing food
- before feeding children or babies
- after handling money
- after handling pets
- after cleaning up after pets
- after cleaning up vomit or other bodily fluids (gloves should be worn when carrying out this activity but hands must also be washed afterwards)
- before sitting down to eat or drink
- after playing outside
- when they appear dirty!

Although long, this list is not exhaustive and you may be able to think of other times when hands need to be washed. It is very important that you discuss, with the children you are caring for, when and why they need to wash their hands and that you encourage them to practice hygienic and healthy procedures at all times (see Figure 2.1). When teaching children how to wash their hands thoroughly, follow these steps:

- Wet hands thoroughly.
- Add soap. Ideally you should use liquid soap as bars of soap can attract bacteria particularly if they are left to sit in water.
- Vigorously massage both hands with the lather. Start by rubbing palm to palm, then rub right palm over back of left hand and vice versa. Interlace fingers, massage the back of the fingers and between each finger and thumb, pay particular attention if you wear any rings and either remove these and wash them separately or wash underneath them while they remain on your finger.
- Rinse hands well, removing all soap.
- Dry hands thoroughly, preferably using a paper towel.

Important

When washing hands you should use water heated to 54°C and the whole process of hand washing should take a *minimum* of 30 seconds!

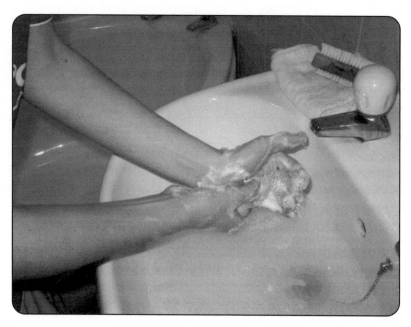

Figure 2.1 It is paramount that children are taught how to wash their hands effectively.
Source: Lee, A. (2008)

Food safety

As a childminder part of your job will be to prepare, cook and serve food and drinks for the children in your care. The way you carry out these procedures is very important as it will not only contribute to the health of the children it will also teach them sensible eating habits. When possible always use fresh produce and encourage children to try a variety of foods. Remember, children's preferences change constantly and while they may not like a particular food one week this may well change if you re-introduce the same food a couple of weeks later.

It is essential that you think carefully about how you prepare, store and handle food to prevent passing on food-borne illnesses such as Salmonella and Listeria, to the children. Young children, in particular, are very vulnerable to such illnesses and it is, therefore, important that you follow good practice at all times.

Storing food

It is essential that you understand the importance of storing food correctly in order to avoid cross-contamination. For example, you should never store raw meat next to other foods in the fridge. Make sure that raw meat is placed at the bottom of the fridge, in a leak-proof container, to avoid blood and other juices, which may contain harmful bacteria, dripping onto other foods. The list below gives guidance as to how food should be stored:

Packets/Cans/Jars – Always store these in a cool, dry place. Check the sell by and use by dates and make sure that the food is consumed accordingly. Many people wrongly assume that dried or canned foods have an indefinite shelf life, however this is simply not true and food in cans should be eaten within 12 months of purchase or by their expiry date. If you are unsure of the 'use by' date throw the food away. Never give food which may be out-of-date to babies or young children.

Canned foods and juices, once opened, must be transferred to a leak-proof container before covering and storing in the fridge. Once a can has been opened, the quality of the contents will be affected, and it is not good practice to store cans, which have been opened, in the fridge.

Salad – Always store salad ingredients at the bottom of the fridge.

Vegetables – Once again, these should be stored at the bottom of the fridge.

Fruit – Although many people understand the importance of storing salad and vegetables in the fridge, often fruit is forgotten and is placed in a bowl left on the table/kitchen counter. However, it is important to remember that leaving fruit out in this way makes it vulnerable to contamination. It is a health risk to leave food out which can be touched by anything or anyone including pets and flies. Think carefully about how you store fruit and always wash it before use.

Refrigeration safety

As aforementioned, it is important that you store food in the fridge correctly. All food should be stored in a suitable, leak-proof container and it should be covered. Fridges should be set no higher than 5°C. Freezers should be set at 18°C. Avoid over filling the fridge as it is essential that air can circulate it to stay cool. Food should be stored in the fridge as follows:

Bottom – this area should be for fruit and vegetables. Most fridges will have a specially designed 'box' for these food items.

First shelf from the bottom – use this shelf for raw meat and fish.

Next shelf up – use this for yogurts, condiments, eggs etc.

Top shelf – use this for storing butter, jars etc. which pose no threat of leakage.

Milk, juices, soups etc. should be stored in the door of the fridge.

Never allow food to thaw out on a kitchen work surface. Place the food in a leak-proof container and allow it to thaw out in the fridge. Make sure that it has completely thawed out before cooking. Once food has been defrosted you must *never* re-freeze it.

Food preparation safety

It is essential that, in addition to storing food safely, you also understand the need for safe and hygienic food preparation in order to avoid infection. By taking note of the following points you will be able to eliminate potential problems caused by harmful bacteria:

• Always wash your hands before preparing or cooking food.

Table 2.1 Risk assessment for storing, preparing and cooking food

Hazard	Risk	Risk rating	Action taken
Wooden chopping board	Cross-contamination of bacteria from raw and cooked foods	High risk	Purchased three colour coded, plastic chopping boards
Fruit left in fruit bowl on dining room table	Contamination from coughs and sneezes, risk of germs from flies etc.	Medium risk	Keep covered or preferably store in the fridge. Wash all fruit before consumption

Source: Lee, A. (2008)

- Never use the same board for cutting and preparing raw meat, vegetables and bread. Always use a separate board for each food. Plastic chopping boards are preferable as these are much easier to keep clean than wooden ones. It is good practice, when preparing food for your childminding business, to use different coloured plastic boards for different types of food to eliminate any chances of cross-contamination.
- As with boards, it is essential that you do not use the same knives, plates or other utensils for cutting or preparing different foods.

It is a good idea for all childminders to look closely at the way they store, prepare, cook and serve food and try to eliminate as many potential health risks as possible. Using a risk assessment chart, like Table 2.1, may help you to spot any dangers.

You may like to produce a simple risk assessment chart like the one above (Table 2.1) for other areas in the home where health and safety factors may be an issue such as the bathroom and toilets.

Food provides an ideal way of transmitting bacteria and infection to humans and it is, therefore, essential that you store, prepare, cook and serve food safely and hygienically if you are to be certain not to pass on any form of food poisoning to the children in your care. Food poisoning is classed as a 'notifiable disease' and it is possible, in extreme cases, usually in the very young and the very old, for death to occur as a result of severe food poisoning.

We are surrounded by bacteria and, indeed we actually need bacteria for our bodies to remain healthy; however, if certain forms of bacteria were allowed access to our food they would multiply quickly resulting in food poisoning. The chart below gives examples of some of the main types of bacteria, their source, the symptoms they cause and how an outbreak can be prevented.

Type of bacteria	Source	Symptoms	Prevention
Salmonella	Found in raw eggs and chicken and the intestines of animals and birds	Diarrhoea, vomiting, fever, severe abdominal cramps lasting from 1 to 7 days	Never store raw and cooked foods near one another in the fridge. Never give raw eggs to children in any form. Ensure that all meat is cooked thoroughly in order to ensure that any bacteria are destroyed

Type of bacteria	Source	Symptoms	Prevention
Staphylococcus aureus	Found in the nose, throat and mouth of humans. Also present in skin, hair, cuts and open sores	Vomiting and severe abdominal pain, which can last up to 24 hours	Wash hands frequently when preparing and cooking food particularly if you have a cold. Tie hair back and cover any cuts or open sores with an appropriate dressing. Avoid touching the nose and mouth
Clostridium perfringens	Found in the soil, it is transmitted via dust, insects and faeces	Diarrhoea and severe abdominal pain, which can last up to 48 hours	Thorough washing of hands before handling food stuffs. Make sure that raw and cooked foods are not stored together and ensure that all food is cooked thoroughly, particularly meat-based dishes
E. Coli	This is the usual bacteria found in the human digestive tract which is transferred by the failure to wash hands thoroughly	Diarrhoea, vomiting and severe abdominal pain which can last anything from 1 to 5 days	Ensure that you practice good personal hygiene methods and that you wash hands frequently particularly after visiting the toilet, wiping noses etc.
Listeria	This is caused by a result of cross-contamination from the environment and can be found in prepared, chilled foods	Listeria is very dangerous to young babies and to pregnant women. Symptoms of Listeria include fever, septicaemia and meningitis	Be careful how you store food and always make sure that your fridge is kept at the correct temperature and that air can circulate. Vulnerable people such as pregnant women and young children should not be given soft cheeses, pâté, or meals, which have been re-heated

Hygienic work practices

Childminders must practice hygienic work methods and, more importantly, they must be *seen* to be doing so. Children learn from the adults around them and it is, therefore, paramount that the children witness, first hand, how you wash your hands, prepare the food, clean up after accidents etc.

Most large settings, such as nurseries will have a policy in place for cleaning equipment and toys, and often they will employ cleaners and caretakers to carry out these tasks. Childminders however, usually work alone and are therefore responsible for the checking and cleaning of all their toys and equipment and you may like to adopt a regular routine to help you to carry out this essential duty.

The chart following sets out some of the common hazards you should be looking out for everyday when you put your toys and equipment away.

It is important that you organize a suitable routine for cleaning your toys and equipment and make sure that you follow this routine methodically if you are to be completely certain that your home environment does not pose a threat to the children you are caring for with regard to health and hygiene.

Material	Signs of wear	Examples
Wood	Splinters Cracks Rough edges Flaking or peeling paint	Tables, chairs, shelves etc. Wooden toys such as dolls houses, jigsaws, vehicles etc.
Plastic	Cracking Splitting Fading of colours	Chairs Toy boxes Toilet seats/potties Bicycle/tricycle seats Tableware, beakers, plates etc. Plastic toys such as rattles, vehicles, etc.
Metal	Rust Flaking/chipped paint	Highchairs, pushchairs, car seats, outdoor equipment such as climbing frames, slides and swings

Toys and play equipment will be handled often by lots of children throughout the course of the day. Remember that babies and young children explore using their mouths and objects will soon become unhygienic if not cleaned properly on a regular basis.

The main areas of a childminding setting, which you will need to pay particular attention to when cleaning are

- toilets and hand basins
- work surfaces
- feeding equipment
- toys and play equipment
- tables and highchairs
- floors
- bins
- potties and changing mats

We will now look carefully at each of these areas and how they can be cleaned effectively.

Toilets and hand basins

These must be cleaned as and when necessary. There is no point telling yourself that you will clean the toilet at the end of the day when the children have gone home, what if someone has had an accident at lunchtime resulting in a wet or soiled floor or dirty toilet seat? Toilets and hand basins must be monitored throughout the day and cleaned when necessary. They should, however, also be thoroughly cleaned at the end of each day. The whole of the toilet, both inside and outside should be cleaned using a strong disinfectant or bleach solution in order to kill the bacteria which inevitably lurks there, with particular attention paid to the area under the rim and the handle!

Work surfaces

As you will be preparing and serving food from the kitchen work surfaces, it is absolutely essential that these are kept scrupulously clean at all times to prevent the spread of infection. Work surfaces should be wiped down regularly with a clean cloth and a suitable disinfectant solution.

Feeding equipment

Babies and young children are exceptionally vulnerable to infection and it is, therefore, paramount that bottles and feeding utensils are sterilized for all babies under 12 months of age.

Toys and play equipment

As I have mentioned earlier, toys and play equipment will be handled often and by numerous children throughout the day. Young children in particular will be prone to putting objects in their mouths and often children taking part in role play activities, for example, using a play kitchen and utensils will pretend to 'eat and drink' the food, often putting them in their mouths. It is essential that plastic items are sterilized – if you have a dishwasher try putting plastic toys in there to be washed, it saves a lot of time and they will be washed at a high temperature. Other items, such as plastic rattles and soft toys can be washed effectively by placing them in a pillowcase, fastening securely and washing them in the washing machine. Larger items will need to be wiped down with a clean cloth and suitable disinfectant solution.

Bear in mind that all toys and equipment will need some form of cleaning and it is a good idea to enquire about the maintenance of an item before purchasing it. If the item appears difficult to clean avoid it. Enquire about the possibility of purchasing spare parts particularly for expensive items which will be prone to a lot of wear and tear.

Tables and highchairs

Many childminders use their dining room tables both for preparing and eating food and for activities such as drawing and play dough modelling and it is, therefore, essential that they are wiped down regularly with a suitable disinfectant solution after each time they have been used. Highchairs should be wiped down carefully each time they have been used.

Floors

Babies and young children will sit or lie on the floor to play and it is essential, therefore, that your floor area is kept as clean as possible. Avoid allowing children and their parent's access to your play areas while wearing their outdoor shoes. Politely request that they remove their shoes at the door and explain that this is for hygiene reasons as you have young children on the floor. Babies should be laid on a mat to avoid soiling the carpet should they dribble or vomit. It is much easier to put the mat in the washing machine than to scrub the carpet! Vacuum your carpets everyday and throughout the day if they become heavily soiled, for example, after a cutting out and gluing activity or following mealtimes. Mop hard floors with a suitable disinfectant solution and make sure that your carpets are shampooed periodically to make sure they are clean and free of dust mites etc.

Bins

Bins harbour bacteria and germs. They should be emptied at least once a day and should never be allowed to overflow. Always wash bins out with a suitable disinfectant solution after emptying and line them with a plastic bag or bin liner. Recycle waste thoughtfully and sensibly.

Potties and changing mats

These must be cleaned thoroughly after every use. Wash potties out with a suitable disinfectant solution. Changing mats should be wiped down with a disinfectant solution after each use.

Disposing of waste materials safely

Although we have looked at how to practice safe and hygienic methods with regard to handling food and cleaning toys and equipment it is also necessary for you to understand the importance, not just of keeping your home and equipment clean, but also of how to dispose of waste materials safely and effectively in order to avoid an outbreak of illness due to cross-contamination from poorly discarded waste products. Waste materials can take the form of

- unused or uneaten food
- soiled nappies
- the contents of potties
- blood
- vomit

Unused or uneaten food

Always wrap any waste food securely in a plastic bag which should be tied before placing in an outside dustbin. Left over food should never be re-heated and served to young children.

Soiled nappies

Always wear plastic gloves and a protective apron while changing nappies (see Figure 2.2). Soiled nappies should be placed in a plastic bag (specially designed gadgets are now available which wrap nappies individually in anti-bacterial film; however, these can prove expensive if you are caring for several children in nappies). Scented nappy sacks with tie handles are inexpensive and highly effective for the disposal of soiled nappies. Always place the nappy in an outside dustbin immediately.

Figure 2.2 Infection can spread easily and quickly in a childcare setting. Always wear protective clothing when changing nappies and cleaning up after a sick child.
Source: Lee, A. (2008)

Contents of potties

Tip the contents of the potty down the toilet. Never be tempted to dispose of urine down the sink! Wash the potty out thoroughly with a disinfectant solution each time it has been used.

Blood

Always wear plastic gloves when treating accidents. Clothing, which has been soiled with blood, should be either washed immediately or placed in a plastic bag, tied securely for the child's parent to take home. Any soiled bandages, dressings, etc. should be placed in a plastic bag, tied and disposed off in an outside dustbin. Any floors or carpets soiled with blood should be washed immediately with a suitable disinfectant solution.

Vomit

Once again, wear gloves when cleaning up after a child who has vomited. Rinse soiled clothes and place in a plastic bag, securely tied for the child's parent to take home or wash immediately according to the manufacturers' instructions. Mop up as much vomit as possible and then thoroughly clean the area with a suitable disinfectant solution. Carpeted areas should be thoroughly scrubbed or ideally cleaned using a steam cleaner to eliminate any traces of bacteria.

The risk of pets

Many families have a pet and childminders are no exception. However, you must think carefully about what kind of pet you are intending to purchase if you carry out your childminding business in your family home. *All* animals can be unpredictable and, even the most friendly of dogs can bite if provoked or accidentally hurt.

Children must be taught to respect animals, to handle them with care and to know when to give them the space they need. Pets are not toys! Before choosing a pet you must take into account the age of the children you care for and their preferences along with the wishes of their parents. There is little point in rushing out to purchase a huge dog which will need a lot of daily exercise if you are caring for a new born baby who needs feeding every 3 hours together with a 2-year-old who can barely walk! Neither is it a good idea to buy a dog if one of the children you care for is apprehensive around this type of animal.

Before purchasing a pet think things through carefully. Weigh up the pros and cons and be honest with yourself about the amount of time you can really afford to give to the pet when you are childminding. It is cruel to purchase a puppy, for example, if you do not have the time to devote to training it, and, the health risks that a puppy who is not yet house trained, poses to young children, doesn't bear thinking about!

Although dogs can be very time consuming and hard work they also tend to be a much-loved member of the family and many childminders have successfully managed owning a dog and running a childminding business.

If you really love the idea of owning a pet, perhaps your own children are desperate for one, but you are unsure of whether you have the time and patience needed to devote to a dog then it might be a good idea to compromise and consider purchasing a slightly less demanding pet, such as a rabbit or guinea pig. Children can be encouraged to care for rabbits and guinea pigs and will learn to be responsible for a pet without having to take it for long walks in the rain!

It is important to remember that all pets, pose some kind of health risk if you do not follow suitable hygiene routines. Children should be encouraged to do the following:

- Handle pets carefully and considerately. Remember even rabbits and guinea pigs can give a nasty bite if they are squeezed too tightly or unintentionally hurt or frightened.
- Take responsibility for cleaning out cages and feeding pets appropriately.
- Wash hands after handling, cleaning out or feeding pets.

Pets can pose a risk of infection and whatever pet you choose you must ensure the following:

- Pets are checked by a vet accordingly and are treated for worms and fleas periodically.
- Pets are not fed in the kitchen.
- Pets have separate feeding bowls from humans and these are not washed together.

- Pets should be tolerant of children.
- They are not allowed on tables or work surfaces.
- Children are not allowed to tease them.
- Children are never left with a pet unsupervised.
- Sick pets are taken to a vet for attention and allowed adequate time to recuperate after they have been ill.
- Any pet 'accidents' are cleaned up immediately and any waste disposed off hygienically.
- Pets should never be allowed to use your outdoor play area as a toilet.
- Exotic pets such as snakes should not be accessible to the children you care for.

It is a good idea for childminders who keep pets to have a pet policy in place in order to be able to reassure parents of their commitment to health and safety measures. Bear in mind that not all children, and indeed their parents, will be as tolerant of animals as you are and you may need, at times, to compromise in some way.

A pet policy for a childminder who owns a dog may look something like this:

Pet Policy

My family and I own a pet dog. His name is Bruce and he is a 3-year-old Border Terrier. Although Bruce is a gentle dog I agree to ensure that he is not allowed into the rooms I use for childminding purposes while I am carrying out my duties.

I will also ensure that I:

- Have my dog regularly wormed and treated for fleas.
- Take my dog for regular health checkups and booster vaccinations.
- Never exercise my dog in the outdoor play areas designated for childminding.
- Never feed my dog at the table or allow his bowls and utensils to come into contact with those used by humans.

Exercise

Write a 'Pet Policy' which you could use for your own setting. If you do not own a pet imagine that you are about to purchase a cat – what kind of points do you think you will need to include for this type of pet?

3 Safety Outside the Home

Although it is essential that you practice effective safety measures at all times while child-minding *indoors* it is equally important that these safety measures extend to your garden area and that you understand the importance of remaining vigilant while out and about. The safety of the children must never be compromised and, as with indoors, supervision is paramount when children are playing outdoors or travelling. Children should be taught the importance of staying safe when outdoors and, while they should be aware of the many dangers posed, they should be informed of these in a sensitive manner so as not to frighten them unduly.

In the past 20 years or so, our streets seem to have become less and less of a 'playground' for children. There are a number of factors for the dwindling numbers of children who are allowed the freedom to express themselves in the great outdoors, one of the greatest factors being the huge increase in the number of cars on the roads today.

By being allowed to play outdoors children not only learn to express themselves freely, but also learn about themselves and the world around them. Many parents today prefer to send their children to organized activities such as dancing classes, swimming lessons, football clubs and judo classes but, while enjoyable, fun and beneficial, these types of 'organized' activities do not allow children the opportunity for creative, self-directed, spontaneous and interactive play which *they* are in control of. Parents seem to prefer the organized classes to freedom of outdoor play believing these are a safer option for their children. The simple truth of the matter is that children will learn to deal with dangers only if they are allowed to take considered risks, which are age-appropriate and supervised.

> **Exercise**
>
> Think of ways in which you could safely encourage children to enjoy playing outdoors. What kind of traditional street games could you encourage? Try to think back to when you were a child yourself, when playstations were unheard of and the main source of entertainment for young children was outdoors. What kind of outdoor play did you enjoy?

Making your garden safe for children

If you are lucky enough to have a garden for the children you care for to play in, it is essential that you ensure that this area is safe and free from any potential hazards. Many childminders, who practice excellent safety procedures indoors, fail miserably when it comes to making sure that their outdoor area is both safe and secure. There are many potential dangers in the garden, which pose huge risks to the safety of a child if not dealt with successfully.

Some childminders use a specific area solely for the use of the children that they care for and, if you have a large garden, this may be an option for you. By fencing off a specific area of the garden, solely to use for childminding, you can be much more certain of keeping this area risk-free and it will then be possible for you to plan the play equipment and planting around the children.

An outdoor play area need not be very big, nor does it need to have lots of expensive equipment, though, of course, if you are in a position to provide swings, a slide and climbing apparatus it is likely that this will appeal to the children! Above all, the garden area needs to be flat, free from hazards, such as water features and poisonous plants and trees, and hold some appeal for the children, be this in the form of a small sandpit and a couple of ride on toys or a huge playhouse and outdoor gym!

First and foremost you will need to ensure that your garden or the area you are proposing to use for the children to play in is free from any hazards (see Figure 3.1). These hazards may include the following:

- **Ponds and water features** – a definite safety hazard which must be addressed. Ideally, your garden will not have a pond or water feature, however if it has, and you do not wish to remove it, then it is essential that children cannot gain access to it. Ponds must be fenced off completely or fitted with a suitable cover which will take the weight of a child should they fall onto it. Mesh and nets are not suitable covers for ponds – they may prevent leaves and debris from falling into the water but they will not take the weight of a toddler if they were to fall onto them.

Figure 3.1 When children are playing outdoors you must ensure their safety at all times. Walls and fences must be in a good state of repair and gates securely fastened.
Source: Lee, A. (2008)

Remember, children can drown in as little as a couple of centimetres of water. Any water butts must be covered securely or ideally removed from the play area.

- **Plants** – make sure that your outdoor area is free from poisonous plants and trees or ones with brightly coloured berries, which may appeal to young children. Plants which should be avoided include

angel's trumpets	hyacinth	poisonous primula
autumn crocus	ivy	rhubarb leaves
castor oil plant	laburnum	rue
daffodil bulbs	lantana	spurge
daphne	leopard lily	thorn apple
deadly nightshade	lily of the valley	wild arum
foxglove	monkshood	winter cherry
glory lily	oleander	woody nightshade
hellebore	poinsettia	yew
hemlock	poison primrose	

(Lee, 2007b)

You would be well advised to make sure that your outdoor area is free from weeds such as thistles and nettles and that you refrain from planting any plants and bushes which may cause scratching, grazing or irritation such as cacti and holy bushes.

- **Drains** – cover all drains with suitable, fitted plastic covers and make sure that children are not allowed to play in or around them.
- **Greenhouses** – these can pose a great danger to children who are at risk should they fall against the glass. Ideally greenhouses should not be situated in the area designated for the children to play. If it is not possible for you to remove your greenhouse, try fencing it off or fitting special film to ensure that the glass does not splinter if broken.
- **Sheds** – children should not be allowed access to sheds. Keep sheds locked at all times.
- **Tools, garden equipment etc.** – these can be very dangerous to young children. Always make sure that you store tools, chemicals etc. in the shed immediately after you have used them and keep the shed locked. If you intend to provide tools for the children to use, purchase ones of a size and weight suitable for the age of the children they are intended for.
- **Dustbins** – never allow children to play in or around dustbins. If possible, remove dustbins from the play area or fence them off.
- **Climbing frames and other play equipment** – a source of endless fascination and a great form of exercise, this kind of equipment can be very useful. However, it also poses a safety hazard if not used correctly. Make sure that all equipment is erected and used in accordance with the manufacturer's instructions and ensure that climbing frames, swings etc. are securely fastened to the ground to prevent them from tipping over. Bark chippings or other suitable ground covering should be provided underneath any climbing frames or swings to cushion a child should they fall. Always check equipment frequently for signs of wear and tear and pay particular attention after the winter months when the apparatus may have seen long periods of inactivity. Corrosion often occurs during this time and you should check carefully for signs of weathering.
- **Washing lines** – never string washing lines across the area where children are playing. Rotary washing lines must be removed or covered to avoid children from becoming entangled in them.

It will be necessary for you to carry out a daily visual inspection of all your outdoor equipment to make sure that it is safe (see Figure 3.2). Regular, thorough inspections should be carried out periodically, the frequency of which will depend on the type of equipment you have, its condition, its history of maintenance, the environmental conditions, the amount of time it is used and the likelihood of any vandalism occurring. You may find it helpful to have a complete record of the inspections and maintenance you have carried out, and these records may prove a useful defence in the event of a claim for injury. An example of an outdoor inspection and maintenance report may look something like this:

Date	Equipment	Comments	Action taken	Signed
16/07/07	Climbing frame	Ladder working loose	Tightened screws immediately – action taken appears to have rectified problem.	
25/07/07	Tricycle	Seat loose	Bolt missing so unable to tighten seat up. Tricycle removed until replacement bolt can be purchased.	
03/08/07	Broken gate	Bolt on fence broken off	Repaired immediately. Also checked fence for any damage – everything appears in good order.	

Figure 3.2 Outdoor toys and equipment must be checked often to ensure they are safe for children to use. *Source*: Lee, A. (2008)

Assessing playgrounds and other outdoor areas for safety

It is good to ensure that your own garden is safe and free from hazards so that children can play without risk, but what happens when you take the children to the local playground or wood for a picnic? How can you be sure that these places do not pose a threat to the children? The simple truth of the matter is that you cannot be certain that the areas are as free from risk as your own personal spaces, largely due to the fact that they are used by so many other people; however, you can do a preliminary check of the areas, *before* allowing the children to play, to make sure that there are no obvious potential dangers lurking. Potential dangers to look for in the local playground may include

- broken glass
- discarded cigarette ends
- syringes
- empty cans and other waste debris

- dog faeces
- spilt food
- blood

Although playgrounds featuring swings, slides and other apparatus can be very appealing to children and they, certainly, provide them with lots of exercise it is, unfortunately, a sad fact of our society that some individuals seem hell bent on vandalizing these areas and using them as places to 'hang out', drink alcohol and take drugs. It is for this reason that you must check any outdoor play areas that you are intending to allow the children to have access to. Before allowing children to use any equipment always

- make a thorough check of the immediate area; make sure that there is no broken glass, syringes, dog dirt etc. before allowing the children to play;
- have a good look at the apparatus for signs of vandalism and, if you are in any doubt, do not let the children go on the equipment;
- carry a travel first aid kit with you when you are out and about in case of minor injuries.

Deciding to take the children on a country walk or for a picnic in the woods creates a slightly different risk to the children. Although there may not be any equipment to check for wear and tear or vandalism there will be other 'natural' risks to watch out for. If possible stick to tried and tested places where you can be relatively sure that you and the children will be safe. Before setting out on a picnic or allowing the children the freedom to play, make a thorough check of the surrounding area. This may not be quite as easy as it is to do in a playground, as the grass may be long, making it difficult to spot potential dangers. Once again, check for signs of unsavoury characters who may have been looking for a quiet place to drink etc. Make sure there are no discarded cans, bottles etc. Other important things to check for when picnicking and enjoying the country side are the following:

- **Nettles, thistles and other weeds** – these may scratch, sting or itch.
- **Dog faeces** – dog walkers get everywhere!
- **Cow dung and sheep droppings** – very much a part of the countryside, but not very pleasant if you sit or stand in it!
- **Barbed wire fences** – these can be very dangerous as young children often do not realize how sharp the barbs can be.
- **Sharp stones** – hidden in the grass, these pose a risk if a child should trip and fall.
- **Rivers and streams** – these can be very dangerous particularly after heavy rainfall when the flow of the water may be fast and the level deep. Always supervise children near water.
- **Animals** – remember that animals are very unpredictable and, if frightened or hurt, they can attack. Teach children the importance of treating all animals with respect and never allow children to go near lambs, foals, calves etc. as the females can be very protective and may be more prone to attack.

Exercise

Take a trip to your local children's public playground, playing fields, woods or someplace where you feel the children would benefit from visiting and carry out your own assessment of the area. Make a note of any potential health risks and whether you feel you can successfully eliminate these problems in order to ensure that the area is safe for the children to play. If you feel the dangers are too numerous to rectify, what should you do?

Collection of children from school

If you decide to provide a school drop-off and collection service, it is paramount that you think things through carefully before deciding which schools you intend to service. You will need to think about the following:

- The proximity of the school/s to your home.
- How many schools/nurseries/playgroups you are intending to service.
- The starting and finishing times of each school, nursery and playgroup.
- How many children you are caring for and their ages. Babies will have specific feeding and sleeping patterns, which may make trips to and from school difficult.
- Whether you will be able to walk or whether you will need to use transport. If you require transport, will this be private or public?

Think carefully if you are considering taking and collecting children from more than one school, as this can be fraught with difficulties. Children must *never* be late getting to class in the mornings and you should never expect them to be hanging around the school gates waiting for you at the end of the day because you are unable to get there on time. You may be able to get there most of the time but what will happen if the traffic is heavy or the weather is bad? It is often difficult during these times just getting to one school to collect children, but if you have to get to two or more and have several children in tow this may be impossible. Think things through carefully before agreeing to any such arrangements and, if necessary, give yourself a trial period to see how things go and whether it is actually possible to service more than one school each day. Of course, you may have some very understanding teachers who agree to keep an eye on the child for you until you turn up; however, if this is an everyday occurrence, they may well tire of such liberties and, of course, you will also need to take the parents' wishes into account. If they are paying you to collect their child from school they may not be very understanding if they discover their child is left hanging around waiting for you for 15 minutes because you have taken on too much business and can't do your job properly!

Things to consider, from a safety point of view, when taking and collecting children from school:

- Never drop young children off at the school gates. Always take them to their classroom so that you can be absolutely certain that they have gone into school. Remember it will be 6 or 7 hours later before anyone would know the child was missing if they were to wander off or, worse still, fall victim to abduction. Schools rarely telephone to ask where a child is as they usually expect the parent to telephone in if their child is ill. Many parents inform the school of the child's absence only after they return to class after an illness.
- Always make sure that children arrive at school on time everyday, and that they have everything with them that they need, such as lunch box, homework etc.
- Always make sure that you are waiting for the child to come out of school and that you arrive on the premises before the bell has gone signalling the end of the school day. If you are collecting different children from different classes, arrange to meet the youngest child outside their classroom (particularly if they are in nursery or reception class) and make sure that all the other children know exactly where to meet you. Arrange with them a suitable place and stick to this arrangement so as not to confuse them. Routine is essential for children.
- If you are going to be unavoidably delayed and you will not be able to get to the school on time always telephone the school to let them know. Inform them about the children you are collecting and make arrangements for the children to remain inside the school building until you arrive to collect them. Never allow children to hang around in the playground or at the school gates waiting for you.

Exercise

Write your own schedule for taking children to and collecting children from school. Record the following criteria:

- The schools you intend to service
- How many children you will have with you
- The opening and closing times of the schools
- The length of time it takes you to get to the school (a) in the morning, (b) in the afternoon, (c) in rush-hour traffic (you may have children to collect later if they have attended after-school clubs etc.,), (d) in bad weather
- Will you be able to do the journey on foot? Will you need the use of a car or will you use public transport?
- If you need public transport, is this available at the times you require?

Finally, after assessing the above points carefully, do you feel you need to change your plans for taking children to and collecting them from school?

Collection from the childminding setting

As a childminder you are responsible for setting your working hours. The times you choose to start and finish work will depend largely on the working hours of the parents who use your service; however, you have the right to expect parents to respect your wishes and, if they have agreed to collect their child at a certain time, and they are paying you until this time, then you should be able to rely on them to keep to their side of the agreement. There may, however, be times when they may be unavoidably late and in such cases you should try to be flexible whenever possible provided this does not become a habit. No one can anticipate a bad accident or heavy snowfalls and these are times when traffic jams will be inevitable, resulting in parents turning up late to collect their children. If parents are going to be late, ask them to telephone you in advance and let you know. This arrangement serves many purposes:

- It is courteous.
- It allows you to make alternative arrangements. You may have arranged to take your own children to a class or you may have enrolled on a training course etc.
- It prevents you from worrying about why they are late.
- It enables you to reassure the child and explain the situation to them.
- It gives you the opportunity of planning activities for the child more easily if you know how late the parents expect to be.

Late collections of children, though sometimes unavoidable, have a 'knock on' effect for everyone else and it is reasonable for you to expect the parents to telephone and explain the situation. If they are going to be very late, perhaps their car has broken down, for example, you may like to ask them to arrange for someone else to collect their child. Always make sure, if parents intend to send someone else to collect their child, that this person is known to you or that they have a 'password' in place so that you can recognize them as being the person the parent wishes to take charge of their child. Never hand a baby or young child over to someone you do not know!

There may be times when a particular parent begins to collect their child late on a *regular* basis and this is something which needs to be handled immediately, if you are to avoid being taken for granted. If you don't say anything, the parent may well think that you do not mind and continue collecting late. They may use the opportunity to stop and fill up with petrol, finish shopping etc. Whatever the reason for being late they will be encroaching on your personal time, and causing unnecessary worry and distress to their child, and this is not acceptable. First, it is important to talk to the parent and find out why they are collecting their child late on a regular basis. Of course, there may be a perfectly reasonable explanation for their lateness in which case you should renegotiate your contract, if the later time is acceptable to you.

Childminders are advised to write and implement a policy for situations when a child is not collected from the setting on time or if they are faced with someone collecting the child who you have not been informed about. Such a policy may look something like this:

Policy for Collecting Children

Please remember that, while I enjoy my job, I do have family commitments of my own, and if, for any reason, you intend to be late, I would appreciate a courtesy telephone call informing me of your delay and the arrangements you intend to make. This prevents the need for any unnecessary worry to both your child and myself and gives me the opportunity for re-arranging my own obligations.

In the event that a child is not collected on time by the agreed person, I would

- continue to care for the child in my setting;
- contact you immediately to clarify the situation;
- if I am unable to contact you, I would contact the next person on your list of suitable people;
- make arrangements for the child to be collected as soon as possible;
- the person named on the contract as the person responsible for payment would be expected to pay for any additional hours for which I have provided childcare at the costs stated in the contract.

In the event of any parents having divorced or separated, please note that I DO NOT have any legal right to challenge either partner should they turn up to collect their child/children. ONLY in the case of a court order having been produced would I be able to refuse permission for either parent to collect the child/children. Should this be the case in your family set-up it is essential that you make things clear both to me *and* your ex-partner as to what is expected with regard to the collection of the child/children.

Always remember that children thrive on routine and consistency of care and, wherever possible, you should ensure that their usual routine is not disrupted unnecessarily, and that parents are aware that some children can become stressed and anxious when not collected on time.

Road safety

The need for teaching good road safety habits cannot be emphasized enough. Practising good habits when walking along the roadside and crossing roads can, quite simply, *save lives*.

Children should be taught to act sensibly when out and about on the street and, when they are old enough, they should learn the 'Green Cross Code':

The Green Cross Code
1 Look right and listen.
2 Look left and listen.

3 Look right again and listen.
4 If it is clear, walk across the road.
5 Keep looking and listening while you cross.

Although children of preschool age are very unlikely to be confident in identifying right and left, it is still a good idea to introduce the Green Cross Code at this stage so that they will become familiar with it over time.

Young children should be taught to hold the hand of an adult for several reasons:

- It is an excellent way of restraining a child.
- It emphasizes the importance of acting sensibly while on the street.
- It makes the child more visible to motorists. Small children can be difficult for drivers to spot. Ensuring that they hold hands with an adult makes them more visible.

It is very important to remember that children under the age of ten should not be allowed to cross a road unsupervised. This is because it is unlikely that their vision has developed sufficiently to judge speed and distance well. It should not be assumed that pedestrian crossings are always safe as, of course, some drivers may fail to stop.

When out and about with young children always follow these guidelines to ensure their safety at all times:

- Use restraints, such as reins, wrist straps or harnesses, or make sure that the child is holding your hand at all times.
- Set a good example for the children. Never rush when crossing the road.
- Talk to the children, explaining to them why you have chosen a particular place to cross and when the time is right to cross.
- Discuss the different kinds of crossings with children.
- If you have a pushchair or pram, never stand with it sticking out into the road while you are waiting to cross.
- Encourage the children to find a safe place to cross and to stand at a safe distance from the kerb while assessing the road before crossing.

It is very important that children are taught that cars do not simply pose a danger to them when they are crossing the road. Walking behind a car, which is reversing in or out of a driveway, for example, is very dangerous. Care should also be taken when walking through car parks. When out and about childminders should teach children to

- use pedestrian crossings whenever possible;
- learn, and put into practice, the Green Cross Code;
- never cross between parked cars, blind spots or bends;
- never mess around with friends on a busy road;
- wear a helmet at all times when cycling.

(Child Accident Prevention Trust, 2007)

Travelling by car and public transport

Many childminders use their own cars to transport the children they care for to school, playgroup, support groups, outings etc. If you opt to use your car for business purposes it is essential that you ensure that it is both safe and practical for carrying out this job. Your car must be large enough to transport all the children safely and each child must have their own seat which is fitted with a secure restraint appropriate to the child's size, weight and age. *Never* try to cram more passengers into your car than you have seats for and never allow any passenger to sit on someone's lap or stand/sit in the foot wells. Before using your car for childminding purposes you must make sure that

- it is safe;
- your car insurance is fully comprehensive and valid for business purposes. The National Childminding Association can advise you about car insurance by telephoning them on 0800 1694486 or visiting their website www.ncma.org.uk (accessed 23 February 2008)
- seat belts are fitted to all seats;
- child locks are fitted to the doors;
- you know how to fasten baby seats securely, making sure that you do not place rear-facing baby seats in the front of the vehicle if it has a passenger airbag;
- when selecting a parking space, make sure that this is in a safe place and that it is possible for children to get out of the car on the pavement side, rather than having children climb out into the road;
- make sure that you are not tired. Be alert and sensible at all times when driving.

If you have been offered a lift by a friend, it is your responsibility to make sure that the car you are travelling in is safe and that the driver is sensible and competent. If you are unsure of the safety of their vehicle, the manner of their driving or the details of their insurance it is essential that you do not travel with them! The safety of the children is paramount at all times.

Although many childminders will have the use of their own cars for transporting children around, there may be times when you will have to use public transport. In an age when most families own at least one car, travelling by bus or train can be a real adventure for young children. If you use public transport regularly, it is highly likely that you will be aware of the times of the buses and trains and where to catch them from. However, if you are more used to travelling by car, but your vehicle is off the road for some reason, then you must prepare for a journey by public transport. Never assume by standing at a bus stop that a bus will pass by within a couple of minutes and, if it does, don't assume it will be the right one! Plan your journey by public transport carefully so that you are aware of all the details such as the correct bus stop or train platform, the expected times of arrival and how long the journey is expected to take. Take into account things such as having young children in tow, crossing busy roads with a pushchair and getting from one platform to another if you need to change mid-way through a journey.

When you are on the bus or train make sure that the children sit with you and are not allowed to wander off through the carriages or down the bus. If the bus or train is busy and there are no seats available, make sure that the children stand next to you and that they are holding on at all times to prevent them from falling. Remember buses stop and start often and the sudden jerking motions can easily unbalance a young child.

Stranger Danger

Very young children are vulnerable to being approached and harmed by strangers, as they are usually trusting and inquisitive by nature. Young children can be easily lured by the promise of a toy or sweets and the consequences can be shocking. Newspaper headlines make for frightening reading and scarcely a day goes by when we do not learn of children being snatched or lured away from their parents, sometimes even taken from the assumed safety of their own homes. The world is a much more sinister place than it was perhaps 20, 30 or 40 years ago, and unfortunately a child's freedom seems to be the price we have had to pay for streets fraught with crime and insecurities. Where once the summer holidays were, for children, a long stretch of weeks exploring, going on picnics and spending the days from sunrise to sunset outdoors with friends, many adults are now much more cautious and prefer to keep their children within sight and hearing at all times trying to guarantee their safety.

Childminders are responsible for the children in their care and they should not allow children to play outside unsupervised. Think very carefully before agreeing to allow older children the freedom of playing outdoors with friends, away from your garden. Even with written permission from the child's parents you will still be held responsible for their safety. 'Stranger Danger' may be a relatively small risk on our streets; however, the risk of other potential dangers such as road accidents, should be sufficient to make you realize that the street is not a safe place for young children and, when you are carrying out your childminding duties, it is essential that you supervise the children in your care at all times.

Although it is vital that children know how to respond if they are approached by a stranger, it is also very important that they are taught how to reduce the risk to themselves by learning a few preventative measures:

- Always make sure that children tell you where they are going, who they are going with and when they are likely to return.
- Always reiterate the importance of steering clear of lonely places such as woodland, quiet lanes etc.
- When walking down a street, make sure that the child knows to walk on the side of the pavement as far away from the kerb as possible – this will prevent anyone from trying to pull them into a passing car.
- Teach children not to speak to strangers – both men and women have been known to abduct children; therefore, children should not speak to either – however kind or polite they appear to be.

- Teach children never to take sweets or gifts from strangers.
- Inform children of some of the ploys which strangers may use to entice them away such as 'I've lost my keys, will you help me find them?' Children can be very innocent and trusting and they may not like to appear unwilling to help out in a case like this. Child abductors are very astute and know the best ways of gaining a child's interest and, ultimately, their trust.
- Although fun fairs, amusement arcades, parks and swimming baths are all fun places for children to visit they are also the kind of places that paedophiles hang around and extra care should be taken if you are allowing children to visit these types of settings, even if you are in attendance.

It is always better that children are prepared for every eventuality. You should never 'play down' the seriousness of child abduction nor should you look to use 'scare tactics'.

What you should teach children to do if they feel threatened

- Make sure that children know that it is alright to make a fuss if they feel scared or threatened. Teach them to scream and shout and attract as much attention as possible.
- If a child has been grabbed, teach them to struggle, kick, bite, hit and lash out.
- If a child has something taken from them such as money or a mobile telephone, teach them to let their possessions go without a fight.
- If a child is in distress and needs help teach them to look for a police officer, traffic warden or any other uniformed personnel. If none are in sight tell them to go into a busy shop and to raise the alarm. Under no circumstances should the child knock on the door of a house or flag down a passing car to ask for help.
- Teach children how to call for help using the emergency services – dial 999.

Protecting teenagers

Although many parents and practitioners accept that young children are very vulnerable and need to be protected from danger, it is important to realize that the dangers do not simply go away as the child gets older and heads into their teenage years. Most childminders will cease to provide childcare for children once they have left primary school and moved onto high school and, therefore, they will rarely come across the problems faced with caring for teenagers. However, if the child's parents work in shift patterns, work particularly late or live a great distance from the school then you may be asked to provide before and after-school care for children of these age groups and you may also be asked to provide school holiday cover. While the vast majority of teenagers can be a pleasure to have around, some can be quite uncooperative and moody!

Teenage children today are faced with a variety of problems such as

- alcohol
- drugs
- street crime

Talk to the children, in a fashion appropriate to their age, and acknowledge their growing maturity. Take into account their need for independence while making sure that they are aware of the many scenarios they may be faced with and help them to understand how to handle themselves. Encourage them to be sensible and to take control of their lives. Peer pressure can be relentless, and many teenagers may feel pressured into trying things, such as alcohol and drugs, against their better judgement.

Anti-social behaviour

However much you care for a child, and you may have been looking after them for many years, there may be times when you may not like their behaviour or you may simply feel that you do not really know who they are. There are many causes for bad behaviour in children and teenagers and sometimes everyday may feel like an upward struggle for you, for their parents and for them.

Factors, which contribute to anti-social behaviour

- an unstable family life
- divorce
- peer pressure
- boredom
- problems at school
- bullying

Although it is relatively easy to list the factors which may cause teenagers to suddenly go 'off the rails' it is important to remember that preventing such behaviour is often much easier than finding a cure for it. It is vital that you keep an open relationship with any teenagers you care for and, even when they are unwilling to talk, make sure that they know that you are there for them and that you can and will help them if necessary. Avoid being judgemental but explain how their behaviour is affecting not just themselves but every member of their family and those in the childminding setting and explain that you want to help them to get their lives back on track. This may not be easy and it can take many months, sometimes even years, but without your help they may never achieve their full potential. Talk to the child's parents and work out together a suitable strategy for dealing with any anti-social behaviour. There is more about managing children's behaviour in Chapter 7.

It is very important, as children get older, that we acknowledge their need to feel competent and capable. Much will, of course, depend on the individual child's age and stage of growth and development, and you must always bear in mind that children mature at different rates; however, it is important that childminders allow teenagers the opportunity to prove themselves. Try not to have unrealistic expectations as repeated failure can lead to frustration and dissatisfaction which will in turn teach the child negative views of their own competence and result in them developing low self-esteem. To enable children to grow into responsible teenagers and adults try to develop their self-esteem and promote a positive self-image by

- offering lots of praise and encouragement;
- providing opportunities to encourage independence;
- always being available to listen when needed;
- allowing children the opportunity to express their personal feelings and wishes;
- allowing children the opportunity to make choices.

4 Accidents and Emergencies

Prevention is always better than the cure. However, it is important to remember that even the most safety conscious of practitioners may find themselves having to deal with an emergency and, it is at these times, when it pays to stay in control of the situation. Having the confidence to draw on your knowledge of first aid will make staying in control all the more easy and it is, therefore, essential that you keep abreast of your first aid training.

Supervision

The single, most effective method of ensuring a child's safety is through constant supervision. Young children should be within your sight or hearing at *all* times if you are to be sure of their safety. Young children are inquisitive and love to explore. They may be surrounded by hundreds of pounds worth of toys and equipment but you can guarantee that, the minute your back is turned, they will be into something totally unsuitable. Given the chance a 2-year-old would much rather wash their doll's hair in the toilet bowl than in the plastic bowl you have provided for such tasks. *You* are responsible for the safety of any child you are providing a childminding service for and it is essential that you supervise the children adequately at all times.

Knowing that you are responsible for the care and well-being of the children is all well and good but what exactly does 'supervision' entail? Supervising children does not mean following them around constantly, giving orders and removing every single item from their grasp 'just in case' it poses a danger. Supervision means that you are *aware* of what the child is doing at all times; that you can either *see* and/or *hear* them constantly.

There can sometimes be a fine line between *supervision* and *suffocation*. As a childminder it is your job to supervise the children in order to ensure their safety; however, it is important that you understand the need for taking into account a child's age and stage of development so as to acknowledge their growing need for independence if you are to avoid *suffocating* or *stifling* their achievements.

Responding to danger

It is all very well to make sure that your home and outside area is free from potential dangers and that you practice safe methods at all times when carrying out your childminding duties; however, it is how you respond to danger that will ultimately make all the difference to the outcome in the long run. Even if your safety methods are beyond reproach, it does not necessarily mean that you will never come across a situation where you will be faced with having to respond to danger and need to make a quick decision. If you go to pieces at the first sign of danger you risk putting the children in your care in even more danger.

All childminders are required, by law, to take a comprehensive paediatric first aid course within 6 months of commencing their registration. The first aid course must be a minimum of 12 hours and this is a requirement of Ofsted (and approved by the agency for nannies, NESTOR). First aid training lasts for 3 years and childminders must keep their qualification up-to-date. The Red Cross and St John's Ambulance run courses, which are specifically designed for people who work with young children.

Exercise

Source a suitable first aid course in your area which would be beneficial to you as a childminder. Find out the dates and venues the courses are run on and who they are run by.

Before successfully dealing with an emergency situation you will need to assess the situation carefully and respond appropriately to the danger. For example, there is no point in rushing in and scooping up a child who has just fallen from the top of a climbing frame. It is essential, *before* moving the child, that you respond to the situation correctly and assess the danger. It may be that the child has damaged their spine in the fall and the very *last* thing you should do in this kind of a situation is move the casualty. Likewise, an accident involving electricity and water could prove potentially fatal to both yourself, the casualty and to others around if you do not respond adequately to the dangers posed. First aid courses are designed to teach you, not only how to deal with a casualty's injuries but also how to respond to and assess the dangers, and we will look at this in more detail later in this chapter.

Personal emergency plans

It is essential that all childminders draw up a personal emergency plan and that all members of staff and children who are old enough to understand, are aware of what is expected of them in the event of an accident or emergency.

You will need to think carefully what you would do in the event of an emergency and have a backup plan in place should you need to take a child to hospital. If you are caring for three children under 5 years old, for example, and one of them has an accident requiring hospital treatment what would you do with the other two children?

When developing your own personal emergency plan you will need to think about the children in your care. You will need to put in place a backup cover and when planning any cover you must bear in mind the number of children you are caring for and their ages. A personal emergency plan may look something like this:

Personal Emergency Plan

I am fully aware that an emergency, like an accident, is unexpected. However, while I cannot *predict* accidents and emergencies, I can be *prepared* for them and I have drawn up the following personal plan to assist me in the event of an accident or emergency occurring during my childminding hours.

- I will ensure that I have access to a landline telephone or a mobile telephone at all times when I am caring for children. When out and about, I will have a mobile telephone which is in full working condition, with me at all times.
- The information I keep for the children in my care, will be updated regularly including home and work contact numbers.
- I will ensure that I have up-to-date information regarding the children's doctor, my own doctor and local police and fire station telephone numbers.
- I will ensure that I have an up-to-date telephone number of my local hospital which has an accident and emergency department.
- I have arranged for a reliable person to be available who can be contacted to help out in the case of an emergency. (You will need to make sure that parents are aware of any emergency backup person you may have enlisted the help of and add their name and contact details to your emergency plan. Some childminders prefer to have a couple of backup people just in case their first choice is unavailable!)
- I guarantee that my first aid training is up-to-date and that my certificate is valid. I will ensure that I attend first aid training every 3 years or as advised by Ofsted.

It is good practice to list the contact telephone numbers of any assistants or other child-minders you work with on the back of your personal emergency plan together with the contact telephone numbers of

- any backup cover you have arranged;
- your doctor;
- your local police station;
- your local fire station;
- your local hospital or the nearest hospital which has an accident and emergency department;
- local district nurses;
- local health visitors.

In addition to the above telephone numbers, make sure that the information you hold for each child in your care is accurate and up-to-date.

It is a good idea to write out the procedure you would follow in the event of an accident or emergency occurring. Furnish each parent with a copy so that they are aware of your procedure and keep a copy yourself; sometimes it can help to have a written guideline to prompt you and prevent panic from setting in. Your procedure may look something like this:

Emergency Procedure

In the event of an emergency I would

- ensure the safety and well-being of any other children in my care at the time;
- assess the injury/symptoms and carry out first aid if necessary;
- telephone for an ambulance;
- continue to assess the situation and administer first aid if necessary;
- accompany the child to hospital if necessary (leaving the other children in the care of my backup person, details of which you have received);
- on arrival at the hospital, or sooner if possible, I would telephone the child's parent/carer and inform them of the situation requesting that they meet me at the hospital as soon as possible;
- telephone the parent/carer of the other children whom I have left with my backup cover, and explain the situation to them. If I anticipate being at the hospital for some time then I would request parents to collect their children as soon as possible. The National Childminding Association only recommends that you leave children in the care of an unregistered person in a real emergency;
- stay with the child until the parent/carer arrives;

If a child you are caring for has suffered any accidents or incidents while in your care you must inform your insurance company and complete the relevant forms.

It is important to remember that, even in an emergency, childminders cannot give permission for medical treatment of a child in their care, regardless of any written instruction to doctors from the parent of the child. In the case of a 'life and death' situation, medical staff will give any necessary treatment. It is for this reason that you must contact parents and inform them of any accident to their child, as soon as possible, so that they are available to give permission for treatment to go ahead. Your contact numbers must be up-to-date if you are to carry out this task efficiently.

Fire drills and evacuation procedures

Schools, colleges and other work places have regular fire drills; however, how many childminders carry out regular fire drills in their own home? If answered honestly, I would expect the answer to this question to be very few! It is, however, absolutely essential that childminder's understand the importance of practising, and more importantly *remembering* to practise regular fire drills with the children in their care. It is probably true to say that most fires in the home are started in the kitchen, and it is paramount that you know exactly how to get out of your home, with the children, safely if a fire were to start on your premises, particularly if your main route of escape is either through the kitchen or by a door which, in order to access, will need you to pass by the kitchen.

Much will depend on the size and layout of your own home when planning your evacuation plan. Many people would expect that a bungalow, for example, would be relatively easy to escape from as, unless it is a dormer bungalow, most of the windows will be on ground level. However, even a house with a layout this simple can pose a great danger if you do not have a personal evacuation plan in place which *everyone* is aware of and which is practiced on a regular basis as; once panic sets in, it will be impossible to evacuate everyone quickly and effectively.

An example of an evacuation plan may look something like this:

Evacuation Plan

In the event of a fire

- do **not** attempt to tackle the fire;
- leave **all** possessions;
- **walk** quickly and quietly to the door (or assembly point you have discussed with the children beforehand);
- file outside and stand on the driveway as far away from the house as possible (or assembly point you have discussed with the children beforehand if your house does not have a driveway);
- **do not** re-enter the building for any reason.

The evacuation plan you produce will, of course, be dependent on the age of the children in your care. Older children are, of course, more likely to want to gather their belongings together as babies and toddlers will have little understanding of possessions. You will need to think carefully about things like assembly points, both inside and outside the house, as these may be dependent on the severity of the fire and its location.

To ensure that everyone understands the importance of evacuation procedures and for them to know exactly what to do in the event of a fire and to avoid panicking, it is essential that you practice your fire drill regularly. Make a note in your diary to practice your fire drill, say once a month. Vary the days and times you practice your drills so that children who only attend part-time will have the opportunity of practising as well. There is little point in planning a fire drill on the first Monday of every month when two of the children you care for attend only on Thursdays and Fridays. Make a simple chart like the one below to record the dates/times of the fire drills, their effectiveness and what changes you feel need to be made.

Fire Drills

Date	Time	Children present	Effectiveness	Changes implemented
Friday 5 October 2007	11 a.m.	Josh aged 2 Amy aged 14 months Katie aged 7 years	Katie wanted to collect her coat and got upset when I told her to leave it behind	Explained to Katie the importance of leaving the building as quickly as possible and not wasting time collecting belongings
Wednesday 7 November 2007	3 p.m.	Katie aged 7 years Suri aged 4 years	Very effective – Katie remembered the importance of leaving behind any possessions	None required

It is very important, when practicing fire drills with children that you reiterate how important it is for them to stay calm and, in the event of a real fire they do exactly as they are asked. The aim is to get everyone out of the building as quickly and safely as possible.

Always make sure that you practice safe procedures within your childminding setting and check your smoke alarms regularly, changing batteries as and when necessary.

Exercise

Write an evacuation and emergency procedure and fire drill which you could use in your own childminding setting.

Caring for sick children

There may be times when you will find yourself caring for a sick child. This situation could come about either because the child has become ill during the course of the day while they are in your care, or they may have been brought to you that morning suffering from an illness which has either got worse during the day or the parent has failed to inform you of.

Childminders are not obliged to care for sick children and you must use your own discretion when deciding whether a child is too ill to be in your setting. When making your mind up you should base your decision on

- the presence of any other children in your care and whether the sick child poses a threat to their health;
- your own health and whether the sick child poses any risk to you;
- the child themselves – if they are clearly unwell and are not enjoying being in the setting, then their parents should be informed.

You would be well advised to write and implement a policy regarding caring for sick children so that everyone is aware of what you will and will not tolerate. Although most parents will put the welfare of their children first and would not expect you to care for them when they are clearly unwell, you may also come across parents who, with no backup cover of their own, and who find it difficult to get time off work when their children are ill, may take advantage of your good nature and bring their children to the setting when they are clearly not well enough to be there. You will get complaints from the parents of other children if you are seen to be caring for a sick child who may pose a threat to the health of the others; in such cases, to protect yourself and your business, you will need to have a policy in place which everyone understands and agrees on.

A sick child policy may look something like this:

Sick Child Policy

In the interests of all the children and myself, I would appreciate parents refraining from bringing their children to my setting if they are suffering from any kind of contagious illness.

By making alternative arrangements for your child and keeping them away from the setting, we can minimize the risk of infection to other children and adults and contain the illness.

If your child has suffered from vomiting or diarrhoea, please keep them away from the setting until a full 48 hours has passed since the last time they had vomited or had diarrhoea.

It is possible that your child may become ill at some time while in my care. In cases such as these, I would contact you immediately if I feel that the child was not well enough to be with other children, or posed a risk of infection, and you would be expected to make immediate arrangements for your child to be collected.

Coughs and colds are an inevitable part of life and all children will suffer from them from time to time. I am willing to care for children with a cough and/or a cold provided they are well enough to enjoy being in the setting and do not have a temperature or are suffering from any other symptoms.

If a child has been prescribed an antibiotic for an illness I would appreciate it if you would keep your child away from the setting for a full 48 hours to allow the medication to take effect and start to work on the infection. Obviously, this does not relate to illnesses such as ear infections which do not pose a threat to others.

Childhood illnesses and diseases are very common, please use your own common sense when deciding whether or not you feel your child is fit to mix with others and if you are in any doubt, kindly telephone me in advance so that we can discuss the best course of action.

I will always make a decision based on the correct action for everyone in my setting.

Get each parent to sign and date a copy of the policy in order to be sure of their agreement and give them a copy to keep.

First aid

It is a condition of Ofsted that all registered childminders are proficient in first aid. Therefore, all childminders must enrol on a paediatric first aid course within 6 months of becoming registered. The first aid course you enrol for must be a minimum of 12 hours in length and include first aid procedures for babies.

All children will suffer from accidents from time to time, some more serious than others, and it is absolutely vital that childminders have some knowledge of first aid in order to deal with these inevitable situations.

While it is essential that childminders are equipped with the necessary knowledge for them to deal successfully with an accident or emergency it is also vital that you know your limitations and, if you are in any doubt whatsoever, you should seek professional advice.

A well-stocked first aid kit, kept out of the reach of children, but within easy reach of adults, is a necessity in every childminding setting.

Your medical box should contain the basic equipment to deal with everyday accidents and emergencies such as

- a first aid manual
- a thermometer
- adhesive tape
- an eyebath
- elastoplasts in assorted sizes
- eye-wash bottle
- safety pins
- several pairs of disposable gloves
- sharp scissors
- sterile dressings in assorted sizes
- sterile gauze
- triangular bandages
- tweezers

Your local authority may have a list of the suggested *minimum* requirements for a first aid box and you would be advised to request this. Keep your childminding first aid box separate from your family first aid box and *never* administer any medication you have purchased for your own children to those you are caring for. Written parental permission must be sought prior to administering any medication or carrying out any first aid procedures.

The primary aims of paediatric first aid are

- to preserve life
- to protect the child from further harm
- to relieve pain
- to promote recovery

It is important to remember that first aid has its limitations. Being proficient in first aid does not mean we are doctors or paramedics; however, it does mean that we have the knowledge to save lives.

Before we look at the types of accidents and ailments a child can suffer from, it is important that childminders are aware of the preliminary stages which can be vital to the outcome. These stages, which you will be taught how to recognize on your first aid course, include

- assessing the situation
- assessing the casualty
- breathing for the casualty
- cardio-pulmonary resuscitation (CPR)
- the recovery position

Assessing the situation

All accidents should be approached with caution. You must stop, think and assess the situation you are faced with before ploughing straight in. Putting yourself and others in danger will do absolutely nothing to help the injured child but may well prove disastrous for them if what you do in the first few seconds is rash and inappropriate. Your own safety is paramount if you are to assist anyone else and this should be at the forefront of your thoughts at all times. Follow these simple steps in order to successfully assess the situation *before* taking any action. Ask yourself

- Are there any risks to yourself or the casualty?

If there are, put your own safety first in order to assist the casualty. If possible, remove the danger from the casualty. If this is not possible remove the casualty from the danger.

Assessing the casualty

When the situation is safe ask yourself:

- Is the casualty visibly conscious? If they have collapsed, try shaking them gently by the shoulders, and talking to them to see if they respond.

If they do respond, treat their injuries (more on this later in the chapter) and, if necessary, call for an ambulance. If you are at all unsure or if the casualty has suffered a head injury always get them checked by the emergency services.

If the casualty does not respond when gently shaken and spoken to then you need to assess how the accident took place and weigh up your options. If the condition is due to injury or drowning and you are not alone then ask the person you are with to call an ambulance immediately and pass on the details of the injured person. If you are alone then it is vital that you do not waste any time. You will need to call an ambulance immediately and, if the casualty is not breathing, you will need to carry out emergency resuscitation. If the casualty is a child you must carry out emergency resuscitation for *1 minute* before calling an ambulance. If the casualty is not breathing you must respond by breathing for them using mouth-to-mouth resuscitation. Your response at this vital time is crucial.

Breathing for the casualty

To carry out resuscitation you need to do the following:

- Gently tilt the head of the casualty well back and check for signs of breathing. This can be done by looking for the chest movements and listening for sounds of breathing. Put your cheek close to the casualty's mouth and feel for their breath. Take up to 10 seconds to check for breathing. If the casualty is breathing then you need to place them in the recovery position while you wait for the ambulance to arrive (more on this later). If the casualty is not breathing then you will need to breathe for them.
- Before administering any breaths you need to open the airway. To do this place two fingers under the casualty's chin and your other hand on their forehead and tilt the head well back. If the casualty is a baby place only one finger under their chin. Remove any obvious obstruction from the mouth by swiftly scooping the object sideways. **Do not** delve into the mouth to try to remove objects which cannot easily be seen.
- Use your thumb and index finger to pinch the casualty's nose firmly. It is vital that the nostrils are tightly closed to prevent air from escaping.
- Take a full breath. Place your lips around the casualty's lips and make a good seal. If the casualty is a baby then place your lips tightly around the mouth and nose.
- Blow into the mouth until the chest rises. It will take about 2 seconds for full inflation.
- Keep your hands in the same position and remove your lips to allow the chest to fall fully.
- Repeat the mouth-to-mouth procedure once more.
- Check the pulse. To do this place two fingers on the carotid pulse in the casualty's neck. If there is no pulse then move onto CPR (more on this later). If a pulse is present continue with mouth-to-mouth ventilation until breathing returns or the emergency services arrive, whichever is the sooner. If breathing does return then place the casualty in the recovery position and keep checking their progress until the emergency services arrive.

Remember

It is important that you do not attempt to resuscitate a child unless you have been specially trained to do so. Call an ambulance if you are in any doubt.

Cardio-pulmonary resuscitation (CPR)

If, after assessing the casualty, you cannot find a pulse or there are no other signs of recovery then you must begin cardio-pulmonary resuscitation (CPR) immediately.

If the casualty is a child of 8 years or above or an adult follow these steps:

- Lay the casualty on their back and kneel beside the person.
- Place the middle finger of your lower hand over the point where the lowermost ribs meet the breastbone.
- Place your index finger above the middle finger on the breastbone.
- Place the heel of your other hand on the breastbone and slide it down to meet your index finger.
- Place the heel of your first hand on top of the other hand and interlock your fingers.
- Lean well over the casualty with your arms straight.
- Press down vertically on the breastbone and compress approximately 4–5 cms (11/2–2 inches).
- Complete 15 chest compressions. You should be aiming for about 100 per minute.
- After 15 chest compressions, give two breaths of mouth-to-mouth ventilation following the instructions given previously.
- Continue alternating 15 chest compressions with two breaths of mouth-to-mouth ventilation.

If the casualty is a child aged from 1 to 7 years follow these steps:

- Position your hand as you would for an adult (see above). However, as the child is smaller use the heel of only one hand.
- Press down sharply this time to a third of the depth of the chest.
- Do this five times at a rate of 100 per minute.
- Give one breath of mouth-to-mouth ventilation.
- Alternate five chest compressions with one breath of mouth- to-mouth ventilation for 1 minute before calling an ambulance and continue with the compressions and breaths while waiting for the emergency services to arrive.

If the casualty is a baby under 12 months follow these steps:

- Place the tips of two fingers one finger's breadth below the nipple line of the baby.
- Press down sharply at this point to a third of the depth of the chest.
- Do this five times at a rate of 100 per minute.
- Give one breath of mouth-to-mouth ventilation.
- Alternate five chest compressions with one breath of mouth-to-mouth ventilation for 1 minute before calling an ambulance and while waiting for the emergency services to arrive.

Quick Check

Adults and children over 8 years – 15 chest compressions at a rate of 100 per minute using two hands on the chest and two breaths of mouth-to-mouth ventilation.

Children aged 1–7 – five chest compressions at a rate of 100 per minute using one hand on the chest and one breath of mouth-to mouth-ventilation.

Babies under 12 months – five chest compressions at a rate of 100 per minute using two fingers on the nipple line and one breath of mouth-to-mouth ventilation.

Remember

The rule for chest compressions and mouth-to-mouth ventilation is

15–2 for someone like you (adult or child over 8 years)
5–1 for a little one (baby or a child under 8 years)

The recovery position

If the casualty is breathing, you should place them in the recovery position while you are waiting for the emergency services to arrive (see Figure 4.1). The following steps take you through the recovery position; however, if you suspect a back or neck injury then the position should be modified as stated.

- Open the casualty's airway and straighten their limbs – place two fingers under the casualty's chin and one hand on his forehead and gently tilt the head well back.
- Straighten the casualty's limbs (but first make sure that they have not suffered any broken bones.)
- Tuck the hand nearest to you, arm straight and palm upwards under the casualty's thigh.
- Bring the furthermost arm from you across the casualty's chest. If you suspect that the casualty may have suffered a back or neck injury, then you must make sure that their head and neck are supported at all times. Place the arm furthest from you over their chest and not under their cheek. If possible get someone else to help you put them in the recovery position so that you can support the head and neck.
- Place the casualty's hand, palm outwards, against their cheek and, using your other hand, pull up the casualty's far leg just above the knee.
- Keeping the casualty's hand pressed against his cheek, pull on the far leg and roll the casualty towards you until they are lying on their side.
- Use your own body to prevent the casualty from rolling over too far and bend their upper leg at the knee so that it is at right angles to their body.
- If necessary make any adjustments. It is important to recheck that the casualty's head is tilted well back in order to keep their airways open. Make sure that the casualty's lower arm is free and lying alongside their back with the palm facing upward.

A child aged between one and seven should be placed in the same recovery position as an adult to prevent them from choking on their tongue or inhaling vomit.

Figure 4.1 The recovery position.
Source: Lee, A. (2007b)

A baby under 12 months should be cradled in your arms with their head titled downwards again to prevent them from choking on their tongue or inhaling vomit.

Important

When dealing with any accident or emergency situation *always remain calm* and follow the 'ABC' method:

- **A – Airway** – Check the mouth for any obstructions
- **B – Breathing** – Check for any signs of breathing
- **C – Circulation** – Check for a pulse

If there is no response to breathing or circulation, telephone 999 for an ambulance and commence CPR immediately. If you are in any doubt The Medical Dispatch Operator at the end of the telephone line will guide you through the procedure.

Common injuries, how they are caused and how to treat them

Choking

Babies and young children usually explore objects using the mouth and it, therefore, goes without saying that you should take care not to allow small objects to come into their reach. Always make sure that children are made to sit down to eat and that babies are never left propped up with a bottle. Never give small children whole nuts, hard sweets or small fruits such as whole grapes.

If your child is choking they will

- have difficulty in breathing
- make strange noises or no sound at all

- appear flushed in the face and neck
- Their skin will begin to turn grey-blue.

To treat a child who is choking follow these steps:

- Bend the child forward.
- Give up to five sharp slaps between the shoulder blades with one hand.
- Check inside the mouth and scoop out any obvious obstruction.

Important

Never put your finger in the mouth or blindly down the throat to try to dislodge an obstruction.

If the back slaps fail, then do the following:

- Stand or kneel behind the child.
- Make a fist and place it below the child's lower breastbone.
- Grasp your fist with your other hand and press into the chest with a sharp inward thrust up to five times at a rate of one every 3 seconds.
- Check the mouth again for any obvious obstruction.

If the choking persists give five more back slaps and, once again, check the mouth for any obvious obstruction.

If this procedure still does not dislodge the obstruction then give up to five abdominal thrusts as described below:

- Make a fist and place it against the child's central upper abdomen.
- Grasp your fist with your other hand and press with a sharp upward thrust up to five times.
- Check the mouth for any *obvious* obstruction.

If none of these methods work you *must* call for medical assistance, dial 999 and continue repeating the cycle of back slaps and chest and abdominal thrusts until the ambulance arrives or the obstruction is dislodged.

If a baby is choking you will need to follow a different routine as babies are much smaller and less robust than children and abdominal thrusts could seriously injure their internal organs.

To administer back slaps to a baby, follow these steps:

- Lay the baby face down along your forearm.
- Keep the baby's head low.
- Give up to five sharp slaps on the back.
- Turn the baby face up on your lap and remove any *obvious* obstruction.

If the back slaps fail to dislodge the obstruction and the baby continues to choke, then give up to five chest thrusts following these steps:

- Place two fingers on the lower half of the baby's breastbone, one finger's breadth below the nipple line.
- Give up to five sharp thrusts into the chest.
- Check the baby's mouth for any *obvious* obstruction.

Repeat the back slaps and chest thrusts three times. If the obstruction has not cleared then you *must* call for assistance. Do not leave the baby unattended, take him or her with you to the telephone and dial 999. Continue to administer back slaps and chest thrusts as described above until the ambulance arrives.

Bleeding

Bleeding can make even the most-proficient carer become unstuck! Often the sight of blood reduces people to a blind panic. Although not always as bad as it may first appear, an injury which results in bleeding needs to be dealt with quickly and the blood flow stemmed.

It is very important that you keep calm in order to reassure the child and that you act quickly particularly if the wound is bleeding severely.

For minor wounds or cuts

- wash the area with clean tap water;
- apply a plaster or dry bandage.

For serious wounds or cuts

- remove or cut the clothing to expose the wound;
- if you have a sterile dressing or pad immediately at hand, then, cover the wound if not apply direct pressure over the wound with your fingers or the palm of your hand;
- if there is something embedded in the wound do not remove it, apply pressure to either side of the wound;
- raise the injured body part above the casualty's heart;
- lay the casualty down;
- apply a sterile dressing over the original pad you may have used – do not remove the original pad – and bandage firmly in place;
- if the blood seeps through the first bandage do not remove it, bandage another pad on top;
- call 999 for an ambulance;
- while waiting for medical assistance to arrive, check the casualty's circulation and, if necessary, slightly loosen the bandage;
- keep an eye on the casualty's appearance and monitor and record their breathing, pulse and level of response.

For nose bleeds

- make the child sit down with their head bent forward;

- pinch the soft part of the nose between your thumb and index finger until the bleeding stops;
- if the nose is still bleeding after 20 minutes, telephone your GP for advice.

Accidental poisoning

As with choking, accidental poisoning can, in most cases, be prevented by making sure that dangerous substances are out of reach of young children.

Young children can easily mistake medicines and chemicals for sweets and drinks, and it is paramount that you ensure that you store all medicines, cleaning equipment, makeup etc. in their original containers and out of reach of young children to avoid accidental poisoning.

> ### Important
>
> If you suspect that your child has swallowed any poisonous substance *do not* attempt to induce vomiting.

If there is vomit in the child's mouth, lay them on their side to allow it to drain away. If the child stops breathing you will need to carry out mouth-to-mouth ventilation as described earlier in this chapter.

Call an ambulance immediately and give as much information as possible about the poison the child has swallowed. While waiting for the ambulance to arrive, monitor and record their breathing, pulse and level of response every 10 minutes. If the child is conscious and has suffered from burnt lips, as a result of swallowing the poison, then offer frequent sips of cold water or milk.

> ### Remember
>
> Take the container of poison with you to the hospital so that the medical staff can see exactly what the child has swallowed.

Burns or scalds

Babies and young children are inquisitive. It is up to you to ensure that the environment they have access to is safe and free from any risk. However, the home contains many potential hazards which may pose a threat from burns, such as

- fires
- hot drinks
- kettles

- irons
- candles
- bathwater
- pans

In the majority of cases, accidents from burns can be avoided. Always make sure that children cannot get access to the kitchen unsupervised and never allow young children near hot objects or liquids. Place the kettle far back on the kitchen work surface and make sure there are no flexes hanging over the edge. Turn pan handles away from the edge of the cooker and always use a fireguard.

Never underestimate the sun's rays and remember that babies and young children can develop serious burns from the sun if they are not adequately protected.

If a child in your care has suffered from a burn or scald, follow these steps:

- Make the child comfortable.
- Pour cold water on the burn for 10 minutes. If the burn is of a chemical nature, increase this time to at least 20 minutes.
- When cooling the burn with water keep an eye on the child for signs of breathing difficulties and, if necessary, be prepared to resuscitate.
- Remove any clothing or jewellery from around the affected area as the injury will begin to swell up, and rings, necklaces, bracelets, shoes or tight clothing may restrict the flow of blood.
- Cover the burn and the surrounding area with a sterile dressing or a clean piece of non-fluffy material such as a cotton handkerchief or a tea-towel. If the burn is to the child's face do not cover it, but keep on cooling the area with water until help arrives.
- Take the child to the hospital or telephone for an ambulance.

Important

Do not burst any blisters or apply any creams, lotions, ointments or fat to a burn. Avoid touching the affected area.

Falls

Young children are very prone to falls. Most children rush around, falling over and banging into things and usually these everyday falls are not a problem. However, if a child has a bad fall you should follow these steps:

- Reassure the child and, if they are old enough, get them to tell you where they are hurting.
- If the child appears to have injured their back or their neck it is vital that you **do not move them**. Telephone for an ambulance immediately.

- If the child is unconscious but you are certain that they have not suffered from an injury to their back or neck then place them in the recovery position, as described earlier in this chapter, and telephone for an ambulance immediately.
- Take the child to the hospital if they have difficulty moving any part of their body or they are in pain as this could indicate a broken bone.
- Take the child to the hospital if they are dazed, are vomiting or if they have difficulty focusing or hearing.

Drowning

It is possible for small children to drown in only a few centimetres of water. *Never* allow children to play in or near water unsupervised.

If a child you are caring for is drowning, follow these steps:

- Remove them from the water.
- Dial 999 immediately and ask for an ambulance.
- If the child has stopped breathing you will need to carry out mouth- to-mouth ventilation, as described earlier in this chapter.
- If the child is breathing then put them in the recovery position and monitor their progress until help arrives.

Allergic reactions

People can be allergic to many things. The main signs of an allergic reaction are

- red, blotchy or itchy skin
- anxiety
- swelling of the face and neck
- puffy eyes
- breathing problems
- rapid pulse
- itching or burning of the lips, mouth or throat
- faintness
- loss of consciousness

Although, most allergic reactions are not serious and will simply result in a little discomfort, others such as nut allergies or bee stings can be very serious and result in anaphylactic shock. Symptoms emerge a few minutes after the child has been in contact with an allergen. This means that breathing becomes difficult, and as the airways swell up it is often impossible to breathe. Children can die from anaphylactic shock and it is, therefore, vital that medical assistance is sought immediately.

> **Important**
>
> If you care for a child who has a severe allergic reaction to certain allergens, make sure that you know exactly what to do should they suffer from a reaction while in your care. It is essential that you know exactly what the child is allergic to and ensure that they do not come into contact with these particular allergens.
>
> If a child suffers from asthma make sure that you have a supply of their medication and that you know how to use an inhaler.

Asthma attacks

Asthma is very common in children. The main signs of an asthma attack are

- difficulty in breathing
- wheezing
- difficulty in speaking
- dry, tickly cough
- a grey/blue tinge to the skin

It is very important that the sufferers are kept calm. Talk to them and reassure them. They can be made comfortable by making them sit up, leaning slightly forward, to make breathing easier. *Never* lay the casualty down. Help the casualty to use their inhaler. They need to take their *reliever* inhaler which is usually blue and *not* the *preventer* inhaler. The inhaler should take effect within minutes. If the attack begins to ease over the next 5–10 minutes then get the casualty to take another dose from the inhaler and encourage them to breathe slowly and deeply. Inform the doctor if this is their first attack or if the attack is severe.

> **Important**
>
> If the inhaler has no effect after 5–10 minutes then you must call an ambulance. Get the casualty to keep using the inhaler every 5–10 minutes and monitor and record their breathing and pulse every 10 minutes while waiting for the ambulance to arrive. If the casualty falls unconscious then you must be prepared to resuscitate, if necessary.

Febrile convulsions

Febrile convulsions are fits or seizures which sometimes occur when a child has a high temperature, usually over 39°C (102°F). These fits or seizures will usually occur between the ages of 6 months and 6 years and they can be quite frightening.

Most febrile convulsions last less than 5 minutes. If a child's seizure goes on for more than this length of time you should call for an ambulance.

Common symptoms of febrile convulsions are the following:

- The child will appear hot and flushed due to their high temperature.
- They will be dazed and confused.
- They may lose consciousness – be prepared for this and make sure that they are not standing up.
- Their muscles will tighten.
- They may moan or cry out.
- They could stop breathing for up to 30 seconds.
- Their skin may turn blue.
- The muscles in the arms, legs, face and other parts of the body will twitch and shake.
- The eyes may roll backwards.
- They may lose control of their bowels or bladder.

Although a febrile convulsion can be quite alarming they are usually short-lived and the child will usually make a full recovery.

To treat a child who is suffering from a febrile convulsion, follow these steps:

- Remove any excess clothing to cool the child down.
- Protect the child from any injury – remove any nearby objects and surround the child with cushions.
- Sponge the child's body with tepid water starting at the head and working down.
- Put the child in the recovery position making sure the head is tilted well back to avoid choking on the tongue or vomit.
- Call for an ambulance.

Important

Never use force to restrain a child who is experiencing a febrile convulsion. Remove nearby objects to avoid injury.

Common illnesses, symptoms and treatment

Diarrhoea and vomiting

Diarrhoea and vomiting are not unusual in children and can often be treated successfully at home. However, if the child shows other signs of illness or does not respond to the treatment you have administered then you should seek medical advice immediately. Children suffering from diarrhoea and vomiting should not be in the childminding setting. Ask parents to keep their children away from the setting for a full 48 hours after the symptoms have ceased in order to ensure that they pose no risk to the other children in your care.

High temperature

A raised temperature indicates that the body is fighting an infection. Normal body temperature is 37°C (98.6°F). If a child's temperature rises above 38°C (100.4°F) and they feel flushed and appear sweaty, then you will need to bring their temperature down to avoid the child being at risk from having a convulsion. You can do this by following these steps:

- Make sure the room is not too hot. The ideal room temperature should be about 15°C or 60°F.
- Remove excess clothing. If necessary, strip the child down to their underwear.
- If the child is in bed use a light sheet rather than a duvet or blanket.
- Sponge the child with lukewarm water paying particular attention to their hands, face and upper body.
- Give the child plenty of fluids. Cool water is ideal.

To take a child's temperature:

Babies – Place the thermometer under the baby's arm and leave it in place for 3 minutes.
Children – Place the thermometer under the child's tongue and leave it in place for 3 minutes.

Children who are suffering from a high temperature should not be in the childminding setting and you should make them as comfortable as possible before telephoning their parents and making arrangements for them to be collected.

Meningitis

Meningococcal bacteria can cause meningitis and septicaemia (blood poisoning). They often occur together. Meningitis is an inflammation of the lining surrounding the brain and spinal cord. Those most at risk are babies, young children, teenagers and young adults.

It is not always easy to spot the signs of meningitis and septicaemia and, in the early stages, the symptoms can resemble those of flu. It is, however, vital that you know the difference and are able to recognize the signs as early diagnosis can mean the difference between life and death.

It is impossible to know when meningitis or septicaemia will strike or whom it will affect. The most common form of permanent damage is deafness; while in severe cases, where septicaemia has occurred, it may be necessary for fingers, toes or even limbs to be amputated.

Common symptoms of meningitis and septicaemia in babies and toddlers include

- fever – coupled with cold hands and feet
- refusal of food

- vomiting
- fretful, dislike of being handled
- pale, blotchy skin
- blank, staring expression
- drowsy – may be difficult to wake up
- stiff neck
- arched back
- high-pitched cry

Common symptoms of meningitis and septicaemia in children and adults include

- fever – coupled with cold hands and feet
- vomiting
- headache
- stiff neck
- dislike of bright lights
- joint/muscle pain
- drowsy – may be difficult to wake up
- confusion

Much has been reported about the rash, which is sometimes present with meningitis. The rash does not fade under pressure when you carry out the 'glass test' as described below.

Glass test – Press the side of a clear glass firmly against the skin. If the rash disappears, it is not meningitis, but if it remains call an ambulance immediately.

Remember

A rash is not always present in the case of meningitis and septicaemia, and it is important that you take into account *all* of the potential symptoms and not simply look for a rash.

Other symptoms of meningitis and septicaemia may include rapid breathing, stomach cramps and diarrhoea. If you suspect that a child has meningitis or septicaemia, it is absolutely vital that you call for medical assistance immediately.

Chickenpox

Chickenpox is caused by the virus *Herpes Zoster*. It is a mild disease which most children will catch sometime during their childhood though it is most common between the ages of two and eight. Winter and spring are the times of the year when the infection seems most common, and usually lots of children are affected at the same time around once every 3 years, bringing about an epidemic.

The patient is infectious from around 2 days before the rash appears until approximately 5 days after. The incubation period, the time from coming in contact with the virus to showing symptoms of the disease, is between 10 and 21 days. Chickenpox spreads through tiny droplets of saliva and nasal mucus coughed out by an infected person and, because the virus is already present in these droplets prior to any rash appearing, the virus spreads quickly.

The chickenpox rash is made up of lots of blisters, which burst and then scab over. Children should not be allowed back into the childminding setting until all the blisters have fully scabbed over – a process which usually takes around 5 to 7 days after the first blister has appeared.

Recording accidents and emergencies

It is absolutely essential that you record any accidents and emergencies, which have occurred to any of the children while on your premises. It is never sufficient to verbally tell a parent that a child has fallen and banged their head, even if there appears to be no obvious sign of injury. Always explain the situation to the parent, write it down in your accident book, sign and date it and get the parent to sign and acknowledge that they are aware of the accident and that they accept the explanation of what has happened.

By law, *all* accidents to children, staff, parents and visitors must be recorded in an accident book. The information you will need to include in your record is as follows:

- The name of the person who has suffered the injury.
- The name of the person who has carried out any first aid.
- A detailed account of exactly what happened.
- Where the accident took place.
- The date and time of the accident.
- The treatment which was administered.

The National Childminding Association sells accident and medication books and you would be well advised to purchase one of these for your childminding business. Pages include space to record existing injuries, this section should be completed if a child arrives at your house with an injury which they have sustained away from your setting, a section to record injuries sustained while on your premises, body diagrams, permission to administer medication and a record of concerns.

Chapter Outline

It is absolutely crucial that all early years practitioners working with children are aware of child abuse and that they consider their own role in protecting children.

Today we are more aware of abuse than ever before and have a very clear understanding of what constitutes abuse and what can be classed as effective behaviour control. For example, in the past beating a child was considered acceptable as a means of teaching a child right from wrong; today most of us would be horrified at this kind of treatment.

What is abuse?

Abuse can happen to any child in any family set-up. Evidence suggests that most abuse is carried out by people known to the children, including members of their own family, friends and sometimes even teachers and carers such as childminders.

It should never be assumed that a child who is from an affluent background is less likely to be abused than a child from a poorer family as this is simply not the case. There are four main types of abuse:

- physical abuse
- sexual abuse
- emotional abuse
- neglect

There are several reasons why an adult may resort to abusing a child and these may include the following:

- The lack of a bond between the parent and child.
- The failure of the parent to respond to their child.
- The failure of the child to respond to their parent.
- An inability by the parent to accept the parenting role.
- Separation of the child and parent.
- Stress and other factors, which may contribute to a lack of interest in the child, such as poor housing, unemployment etc.
- Parents who have been victims of abuse themselves.

Physical abuse

Physical abuse is the intentional infliction of an injury on a child by an adult or the failure to prevent the infliction of injuries by another adult. Physical abuse may take the form of

- hitting
- shaking
- burning
- biting
- using excessive force when feeding
- giving drugs or alcohol

It is important to remember that all children will experience some form of accidental injury throughout their childhood years and they may well experience cuts, bruises, bumps and even broken bones. The differences between genuine accidents and deliberate acts of physical abuse are

- the location of the injury
- the frequency of the injury

The location of the injury

Accidental injuries to children usually occur on the following parts of the body:

- forehead
- chin
- nose
- knees
- elbows
- forearms
- spine
- hips
- shin

The following areas are common sites for *non-accidental* injuries:

- lips and mouth
- eyes
- ears
- cheeks
- skull
- chest
- stomach
- buttocks
- back of legs
- upper and inner arms
- genital areas
- rectal areas
- soles of the feet
- neck

It is very rare for a child to sustain an accidental injury to the neck. Equally, a torn Frenulum (the tongue attachment) should be viewed with suspicion. Haemorrhages to the earlobes are also rarely accidental as are *two* black eyes, particularly if there are no other apparent injuries to the head or face. You should always be concerned if a child's injuries appear to be of an unusual shape or give a clear indication that the child has been hit with an instrument such as a belt.

The frequency of the injury

Physical injuries are, sometimes accidentally, common in children, and a child who appears to have a history of age-appropriate injuries should not automatically raise suspicion of child abuse. Suspicion should, however, be raised if a child appears to suffer from the following:

- Varying injuries sustained over a period of time – for example, bruises of differing colours would imply that a child has been subjected to injury over a period of time.
- Illnesses which cannot be accounted for such as recurring stomach pains or headaches.
- Appearing to succumb to more than an average amount of accidents for which there is no explanation for the injury.

There are both physical and behavioural indicators attached to a child who is suffering from this type of abuse and practitioners need to be aware of all the signs. As I have said previously, all children will, at some point, succumb to accidental injury through everyday play. Some children are more accident prone than others and some are simply clumsy! It is always a good idea to talk to children about their injuries – children who have had a genuine accident are usually forthright in their explanations and enjoy recalling the incident for avid listeners. Suspicion should be raised if children are reluctant to talk about their accident or if they appear nervous or upset, as this may be a sign of the abused children having been warned by their abuser not to talk about their injuries and they may feel confused or uncomfortable about what, if anything, they should say. In addition to the physical signs an abused child may suffer from, this type of abuse also results in behavioural indicators such as

- aggression towards other children or when playing
- showing signs of not wanting to be with certain people
- appears shy and withdrawn
- appears to be in pain

Sexual abuse

Sexual abuse is when an adult uses a child for their own sexual gratification. Sexual abuse covers a wide range of acts such as the following:

- Being exposed to sexually explicit photographs, videos or webcams.
- Encouraging a child to take part in any form of sexual activity including stripping or masturbation.
- Failure by the adult to take adequate measures to prevent a child from being exposed to sexual activity.
- Genital or oral stimulation.
- Indecent exposure.
- Meeting a child following sexual 'grooming' with the intention of carrying out abuse.
- Rape.
- Sexual fondling of any part of the body either clothed or unclothed.
- Sexual intercourse.
- Taking, making or permitting to take, distributing, showing or advertizing indecent images of children.

The physical signs associated with sexual abuse will, of course, usually be confined to the genital areas and, unless the child is at an age where they need assistance when visiting the toilet, these signs may be difficult for practitioners to detect. However, it is important to be aware of the physical signs associated with sexual abuse and these include the following:

- Bloodstains in underwear.
- Difficulty in going to the toilet and showing distress when needing to pass urine or have a bowel movement.
- Difficulty sitting down or moving about.
- Frequent 'accidents' when the child wets or soils themselves.
- Frequent infections of the genital areas.
- Non-accidental bruising or scratching particularly around the genital areas.
- Vaginal discharge.

Sexual abuse can be very difficult to detect, particularly, as many children do not appear to show many 'outward' physical injuries. However, although the physical signs may not be apparent, the behavioural indicators should be much easier to detect and these may include the following:

- Appearing depressed or withdrawn.
- Avoiding being alone with certain people.
- Dropping hints or clues to try to tell you what is happening to them – this is known as a covert disclosure.
- Exposing the genital area.
- Losing interest in school and starting to perform badly in school work.
- Masturbating in public.
- Painting or drawing images of a sexual nature.
- Resorting to immature comfort behaviour such as rocking or thumb sucking not usually associated with a child of that age.
- Showing insecurity.
- Showing unexpected fear of certain people.
- Undressing themselves at inappropriate times.
- Using imaginary play to act out behaviour of a sexual nature.
- Using sexual behaviour not usually associated with a child of that age.
- Using sexual language not usually associated with a child of that age.

Most sexual abuse is carried out by someone known to the child and, in many cases it occurs during normal, routine family activities such as during bath time or at bed time and, therefore, the child may be quite oblivious to what is happening and does not always realize that anything unusual is occurring. However, other children, who will understand that what is happening is wrong, may be threatened into keeping the activity a secret; they may be told that they will break up the family or be taken into care if they disclose the secret and many children are even made to believe that the abuse they are experiencing is a direct result of their own behaviour and that they have 'caused' it to happen, adding guilt to an already very confused child's mind.

Emotional abuse

Emotional abuse is when children are refused love and affection. The adults caring for them may regularly threaten them, shout at them, ridicule or verbally abuse them. The result of emotional abuse is a child lacking in self-confidence and feeling unworthy of love and affection. Children suffering from emotional abuse may find it difficult to form lasting relationships in later life as a result of the long-term effects of the abuse.

Some children, who have suffered from emotional abuse, may resort to self-harm such as trying to cut or mutilate themselves in some way; however, usually there are very few physical signs of emotional abuse. The main indicators of this type of abuse are behavioural and these include the following:

- Trying too hard to please other people in an attempt to feel accepted.
- Being fearful of new people and situations.
- Being unable to trust people.
- Becoming anxious.
- Becoming passive.
- Becoming uncooperative and attention seeking, perhaps resorting to telling lies and becoming 'clingy' towards certain adults.
- Developing speech impediments such as stuttering and stammering.
- Finding it difficult to accept praise.
- Lacking in self-esteem.
- Developing poor social skills and finding it difficult to mix with other children of a similar age.
- Regressing with toilet training.
- Resorting to comfort-seeking behaviour such as thumb sucking or rocking.
- Resorting to stealing.
- Resorting to tantrums due to frustration and a lack of acceptance.
- Showing aggression.
- Suffering from an all round delay in their development.
- Suffering from lack of concentration or lose interest in the things around them.

It is important to remember that emotionally abused children are also at risk from sexual abuse as they crave love and affection and may look for this from strangers.

Neglect

A child who does not receive the basic care they need to thrive is said to be suffering from neglect. Neglected children do not receive sufficient food, warmth and supervision and are often denied basic medical treatment. Often children who are neglected are actually loved;

however, their parents or carers may be suffering from personal problems or they may simply lack the necessary knowledge required to provide for their offspring. Neglected children may also have parents who are suffering from some form of mental illness or who are drug users. Neglected children will show both physical and emotional signs. Physical signs may include the following:

- The child appearing unkempt, dirty and smelly.
- The child being underweight.
- The child not having adequate clothing suitable for the time of year.
- The child suffering frequent injuries due to a lack of supervision or adequate safety devices.
- The child suffering from minor infections and ailments on a regular basis which go untreated such as earaches, coughs and toothache.
- The child appearing to be constantly hungry.
- The child being tired due to lack of sleep or irregular sleeping habits.
- The clothing the child does have may be dirty and unwashed and will often be ill-fitting.

Neglected children may show the following behavioural signs:

- Talking about being left alone to fend for themselves or being in charge of younger siblings.
- Acting responsible beyond their years, perhaps young children appear knowledgeable in cooking and caring for others which is not normally associated with a child of their age.

Helping children to protect themselves against abuse

Although, adults can, and should, do many things to safeguard the children in their care; it is also necessary for children to learn how to protect themselves from abuse. Children should be taught how to protect themselves in a sensitive, age-appropriate manner without resorting to scare tactics. Although much of the responsibility for protecting children lies on the shoulders of the adults caring for them, we must ensure that children learn some basic rules about how they can be responsible for their own safety and how they can protect themselves from abuse. Children should be taught to understand that

- It is not always appropriate to be polite and courteous to adults. Although, this advice will go against many things you have taught a child with regard to acceptable behaviour it is necessary for children to understand that they have rights and, if an adult is showing unacceptable behaviour towards them, they do not have to accept it simply because they are children.
- All too often children are led to believe that they must 'do as an adult tells them'. This advice is a bit like being polite and courteous towards adults at all times and should only really take effect if the child is being shown the same consideration by the adult. Children should be taught that they have the right to say 'no' to something which they are unsure of or if something is worrying or frightening them. Children must be taught to understand that they can refuse to do anything which they are uncomfortable with.

- Once again, when teaching children acceptable behaviour we often tell them not to 'answer back', 'argue', 'shout' or 'kick up a fuss'. When teaching children how to protect themselves from abuse the very opposite is true! Children who feel threatened should be taught to make as much noise as possible; they should be encouraged to scream, shout and kick out if necessary.

Children can be taught, successfully, how to protect themselves if the adults doing the teaching are prepared to do so in a calm and patient manner and by using age-appropriate language and tactics. Adults need to listen to the children and help and encourage them to make the right decisions and choices. It is important to offer guidance and show respect towards the child in order to build on their confidence and self-esteem.

Children should be encouraged to learn about their bodies. Adults need to ensure that children are aware of who should be allowed to touch them, for example, doctors and the reasons behind this. Children should be encouraged to respect their own bodies and be confident in their knowledge of what is and is not appropriate behaviour.

To enable children to stay safe they should be taught the following:

- How to respond to unwanted attention or inappropriate behaviour towards them.
- What to do if they get lost when away from home or the childcare setting.
- About the dangers of talking to people they do not know and how to respond if they are approached by a stranger.
- That it is alright to tell someone if they are worried or concerned and that keeping a 'secret' is not always the right thing to do. Children need to know that they should not feel guilty about breaking a confidence or telling a secret.
- Who they can turn to if they need help and advice and they need reassurance that this person will listen and respond accordingly (see Figure 5.1).

Childminders and other early years practitioners can play an active part in protecting children from abuse by

- listening to what the children have to say;
- being aware of the signs and symptoms of abuse and neglect;
- understanding their setting's procedures and being confident in their knowledge to act on suspicions of abuse should the need arise;
- ensuring that any assistants or co-childminders they work with have no criminal convictions relating to children and taking all reasonable steps to ensure that any employees they take on are suitable to be in contact with children;
- understanding the rights of children;
- providing activities and opportunities to promote self awareness;
- carrying out routine observations.

Abuse of children with disabilities

Disabled children can be very vulnerable to abuse largely because they are not always capable of communicating adequately and, therefore, disclosing their suffering. Sadly, paedophiles

Figure 5.1 Talking to children and helping them to explore their emotions will make it easier for them to tell you anything which is upsetting them.
Source: Lee, A., (2008)

and other predators see this as a way of concealing their actions and, therefore, they prey on the most vulnerable of children.

Often children with learning disabilities appear much younger than their actual age and their disability may make them less aware of what is and is not viewed as acceptable behaviour in public.

Although, sometimes, it is often difficult to know whether a disabled child has suffered from abuse this does not mean that the possibility can be overlooked and you should never dismiss any worrying signs as simply being an inevitable consequence of their disability. If you have any concerns, but are uncertain about the signs, always ask yourself how you would feel and react if the child in question did not have a disability, which could be used to explain their behaviour.

The fact that disabled children may require more personal physical care and they may, at times, have been subjected to continual intrusive medical procedures, makes them even more vulnerable to abuse. They may find it difficult to differentiate between medical treatment and abusive exploitation and they may end up believing that all intrusive attention is normal and necessary.

Disabled children who have difficulty communicating may find it impossible to disclose what they are experiencing and, of course, those suffering from a high level of disability may be completely helpless and unable to resist their abuser.

As a parent or carer of a disabled child, it is paramount that you keep a close eye on everything the child does. You need to be sure that the medical attention they receive is appropriate and never be afraid to ask questions about medical procedures you are unsure of. Depending on the severity of the child's disabilities you will need to encourage them to take as much responsibility as possible for their own care and explain to them who is and is not responsible for helping them with their intimate needs so that they know that only one or two people are in a position to assist them in this way. Remember, all children have a right to privacy and respect.

Disabled children are open to abuse in a variety of ways such as

- confinement
- discrimination
- force feeding
- isolation
- lack of privacy
- physical restraint
- sedation
- segregation
- sexual abuse

It is often much more difficult to spot the signs of abuse in disabled children as sometimes, parents and carers, tend to put down any changes in behavioural patterns or mood swings to the disability. However, those who are involved in the care of a disabled child will get to know them well over a period of time and should be just as aware of any patterns of change in their behaviour as they would in any able-bodied child. As a childminder of a disabled child your suspicions should be immediately aroused if the child shows

- any unexpected fear towards an individual or appears reluctant to be near them
- signs of any unexplained or repeated injuries such as bruises, cuts and grazes
- signs of eating problems
- signs of sleeping problems
- signs of inappropriate sexual behaviour or awareness of sexual activity
- signs of self-harming
- signs of unusual aggressive behaviour
- signs of unusual withdrawn behaviour

There are certain things that parents and carers of disabled children can do to protect them such as the following:

- Listening to children and taking on board everything they tell you. Never dismiss their feelings.

- Talking to the child. Making sure that they are happy with the care and medical treatment they are receiving and always taking their own wishes and feelings into account. A disabled child is no less needy of love and reassurance than any other child and they have the right to privacy and for their feelings and opinions to be taken into account.
- Using props and other resources to enable the child to communicate successfully with you if they have a speech problem. If necessary childminders should learn sign language to enable them to communicate with disabled children and the use of pictures and other resources can be invaluable.

Disabled children are probably more in need of love and affection than other children as they are often prone to depression and feelings of inadequacy. Encourage children to feel good about themselves and, instead of dwelling on the things they have difficulty doing, try focusing on the things they are good at and offer lots of praise and encouragement to boost their confidence and enable them to feel proud of their achievements.

Childminders should provide positive images of disabled people in the setting such as showing pictures of people with disabilities in successful roles such as teachers, politicians, musicians and entertainers. Never let yourself see the disability before the child.

The legal framework for protecting children from abuse

It has now been established, by law, that children have rights and this has been made clear by the introduction of The Children Act 1989 which sets out that children have a right to basic standards of care, nurture and upbringing. The emphasis heavily states that parents have *responsibilities* towards their children and not rights over them. In addition to this Act, the United Kingdom signed the United Nations Convention on the rights of the child in 1991 and this convention sets out three main rights that children are entitled to have and should be taken into account when decisions are being made about them. These rights are

- best interests
- non-discrimination
- views of the child

Best interests

This right refers to decisions being made by adults or organizations and states that any decisions made which affect the child must be done in a way which takes into account what would be the best outcome for the child.

Non-discrimination

This right refers to all children being treated equally regardless of their race, religion, language, disability or family background.

Views of the child

This right takes into account that children have the right to an opinion on anything which affects them.

In addition to the above main rights, the United Nations Convention also recognizes the following rights:

- Access to information
- Civil and political rights
- Freedom of expression
- Freedom of thought, conscience and religion
- Name and nationality at birth
- Privacy
- Protection from harmful treatment
- Protection from violence

Caring for children who have been abused

As a childminder you may find yourself working with a child who has been a victim of abuse. You will need to be confident in your approach to caring for children who have suffered abuse in the past, and it is essential that you understand the importance of accessing relevant training and liaising with other professionals working with the child in order to provide the best possible care and to ensure that everyone working with the child is using appropriate and agreed strategies. Children who have been abused may show a whole spectrum of emotions and behavioural traits such as

- anger
- fear
- resentment
- confusion
- guilt
- hostility
- mood swings
- stress

The child may switch from being calm and co-operative to being abusive and disruptive. They may 'act out' their experiences in the setting and may have little understanding of what is classed as appropriate and inappropriate behaviour in public. As a childminder working with an abused child you will need to be patient and understanding and give the child the time and space they require to enable them to trust you. It may take a long time for you to help build their confidence and for the child to feel happy and secure in your care and, of course, this is understandable. Abused children have quite simply been let down in the worst possible way by adults whom they have trusted and it can take many years for a child to overcome their feelings of betrayal.

Monitoring, assessing and recording abuse

Keeping records is a vital part of any childminding business and never has this been more important than when dealing with matters of child abuse. Your monitoring, assessing and recording must be accurate and factual. Never record assumptions or opinions and always make sure that only the relevant information is included. All records must be kept in a secure place and must remain confidential on a 'need to know' basis. By this we mean that only the adults who are directly involved in working with the child should have access to their records.

It is quite natural for childminders to have feelings of fear and apprehension if they are faced with a possible case of child abuse. You may have suspicions but feel unsure whether the evidence you have is sufficient and be apprehensive that you may be completely wrong in your conclusion. You may also have feelings of disloyalty towards the parents of the child and may be fearful of 'jumping to the wrong conclusions'. However, it is vital that you remember that you have an obligation to consider the safety and the welfare of the child at all times and that you must report your concerns in a professional and confidential manner.

If you suspect that a child in your care is being abused or neglected you will need to decide whether it is appropriate initially to speak with the parents. Your decision about whether to speak with the parents should be based on the nature of your suspicions and, if by talking to the parents you feel you may be putting the child at greater risk, you should refrain from doing so.

Childminders have two choices for reporting suspected cases of child abuse; they can either

- contact their local authority
- contact the National Society for the Prevention of Cruelty to Children (NSPCC)

Both social services and the NSPCC have the power to investigate any report you may make. The child, their parents and yourself will all be spoken to about your concerns and the case will be investigated. You will be asked to provide your record of concerns and the information you supply may be crucial to the result of the case.

A good way of recording concerns of child abuse or neglect is to use a diary style record or a standard form, which can be completed on a regular basis. Either method is acceptable provided it is factual and includes important, relevant information such as

- the date
- the time

- what you have observed
- what the child has said
- how you have responded

Your records need to be

- legible;
- confidential;
- up-to-date – records must be completed within 24 hours of a suspected incident or earlier if possible while the event is fresh in your mind and you are confident about what the child has said.

Always remember that if, when you have reported a suspected case of abuse, the professionals involved decide to investigate the matter, your records will be vital evidence and, as such, they must be accurate. It may be many months after the event has taken place when you are questioned on the incident and it is, therefore, important that you record all relevant information at *the time* rather than rely on your memory later on.

Once you have reported your suspicions to either social services or the NSPCC the usual procedure of investigation will be carried out along the following lines:

Childminder suspects a case of abuse.

If appropriate, the childminder speaks to the child's parents about their concerns. If this course of action is not appropriate, then the childminder contacts social services or the NSPCC to report their concerns.

Social Services or the NSPCC will then collect all relevant information from the people involved in the case.

A case conference will take place to discuss the best interests of the child. The childminder will usually be included in this conference.

An action plan will be agreed.

A case conference is a way of getting together parents, social workers and other professionals, such as doctors, teachers etc. and pooling together all relevant information about the child's situation and well-being.

Whenever possible children will be brought up within their own family setting in accordance with The Children Act 1989; however, sometimes, in extreme cases, children may be removed from their family set-up and taken into care. However, a court must be completely satisfied that there are sufficient grounds before such a decision is made. Usually a court will decide on whether or not to grant an order for a child to be taken into care based on

- whether a child is likely to suffer significant harm if they remain in the care of their family
- whether the child is beyond parental control

There are five types of child protection orders which can be applied for by social services and the NSPCC and these are

A child assessment order – this type of order is usually requested to allow professionals to assess a child, particularly in a case, where the parents have refused permission for their child to be checked. A child assessment order can only last for a maximum of 7 days.

An emergency protection order – this type of order is issued when it is considered necessary for a child to be taken into care immediately. An emergency protection order can only last for a maximum of 8 days.

A recovery order – this type of order is issued to a person who has abducted a child or if the child is part of a family fleeing from the local authority. A recovery order demands that the child is brought forward.

A care order – this type of order places the child in the care of the local authority and parental responsibility is shared between the child's parents and the authority. This type of order lasts until such time as a court discharges it or the child reaches the age of 18 years.

A supervision order – this order places a child under the supervision of the local authority while remaining in their own home. A supervisor is given the job of advising and assisting the child and can make arrangements for any necessary medical treatment. Supervision orders last 1 year after they have been made; however, they can be discharged earlier or, in some cases, even extended.

Understanding the boundaries of your role as a childminder

Childminders need to understand that child abuse is very serious and they must never try to deal with such matters on their own. A child suffering from abuse is very vulnerable and professional help and advice is essential. Despite your fears of being mistaken or of making false accusations, it is absolutely paramount that you report your suspicions to the appropriate professionals. Trying to deal with matters yourself by talking to the parent, for example, may put the child at even greater risk and by encouraging a child to confide in you by asking them questions or prompting them can be seen as interfering with evidence and, should the case go to court, your influence in this way, however well meaning, may seriously damage the outcome.

As a childminder the best way you can help a child who you suspect is being abused is to follow the procedures set out by your own Local Safeguarding Children Board (LSCB) which was previously known as the Area Child Protection Committee (ACPC) or the NSPCC. Record your suspicions accurately and factually and then allow the professionals who are adept at handling these situations do their job.

Seeking support for yourself

As a childminder who may have had to deal with a suspected case of child abuse, you may find yourself experiencing a mixed array of emotions. You may feel

- angry
- confused
- devastated
- guilty
- disgusted
- afraid
- shocked

All of these emotions are perfectly natural; however, it is very important that you try to keep your feelings to yourself when a child is telling you about their experiences. Never let the child see how shocked or disgusted you feel as this will compound and add to their own feelings.

Exercise

How would you feel if you were confronted with a case of child abuse? Make a list of the emotions you think you would experience if you discover that a child in your care has been physically abused.

Child abuse is a very sensitive topic, and it is likely that you will experience a great range of emotions if you are caring for a child who is or has been abused. You may, at times, feel responsible for what has happened to the child and be of the opinion that you have failed them by not being able to protect them from the abuse they have suffered.

You should not be expected to deal with these emotions by yourself. However, you need to consider your position and deal with the situation in a professional manner. Remember that you have a duty to the child and you must maintain confidentiality at all times despite needing the support of others. There are a range of other professionals that you can contact in cases such as child abuse and they will be able to offer the support you may need:

- Child protection police officers
- Health visitors
- Network co-ordinators
- Social workers

6 Bullying

Bullying is a form of abuse which can be carried out by both adults and children. Bullying can take on many forms; however, all usually result in distress and emotional problems for the child concerned. Bullying is *never* a form of harmless fun. It is completely unacceptable and must be stopped immediately.

The bully

Often people who resort to bullying do so because of their own insecurities and feelings of failure. By inflicting pain or emotional suffering on another person it can often make a bully feel better about themselves. Although much of our sympathies when dealing with incidents of bullying will, quite rightly, lie with the victim, it has to be said that the bully themselves also need help and, to provide this, we need to know why certain people feel they have to inflict suffering on others. Often bullies will work in groups and pick on individuals who are smaller or more vulnerable than themselves in order to increase their own sense of power and authority.

Bullies, like their victims, are in need of help. However, before being able to help a person who resorts to bullying, we need some insight into why they are behaving in this way. Reasons for their behaviour are not *excuses*; however, by trying to understand what makes a bully 'tick' and taking steps to understand their behaviour it will assist practitioners enormously when trying to help them. There are many reasons why some children resort to bullying:

- Being ignorant about what is and is not acceptable behaviour. Some children have absolutely no conception whatsoever about how they should and shouldn't behave and as a result they have no understanding of how to limit their demands or indeed why it is necessary to do so. This kind of behaviour may come about as a result of a child being denied any form of indulgence themselves by their own parents and the child has, therefore, come to recognize that by using threats and intimidation they are more likely to achieve what they want or, at the other end of the spectrum, some children, who have been spoilt and indulged excessively by their parents, may resort to bullying because they are so used to demanding their own way and have never been taught how to limit their behaviour. Subsequently, they expect everyone to give into their demands, resorting to harassment if necessary.
- The child may have actually been a victim of bullying themselves. Although most of us would expect that a victim would be less likely to inflict the kind of pain and suffering on another person that they themselves have endured, sadly this is not always the case. Often victims will 'turn the tables' and resort to bullying themselves either because they feel it is 'pay back time' or because they consider that by becoming the aggressor themselves they are less likely to be the victim.
- Children who have been abused in the past by adults may have difficulty understanding how to behave towards their peers and they will resort to abusive, bullying behaviour.
- Being part of a group can often trigger bullying as each member of the group competes for attention and aims to stake their position as 'top dog'. Bullies need to be accepted by their peers and will try to impress others with their abusive behaviour. Other members of the group may be reluctant to stand up to the bully for fear of recrimination and often group members will go along with the leader to remain in favour and maintain their identity within the group.
- Bullying makes people feel powerful. Often children with low self-esteem and little confidence will resort to bullying as a way of making themselves appear influential, strong and formidable.
- A fall out amongst friends. Bullies are often former friends of their victims.
- Family problems can sometimes result in a child bullying others as they may feel insecure, unloved and full of self-doubt, and bullying others increases their sense of importance.

The victim

Any child can be a victim of bullying; although, more often than not victims are selected because they appear outwardly different to their peers. For example, a child with red hair, or who wears glasses may be victimized by name-calling as can someone with coloured skin or an obvious disability.

Children usually experience bullying at school though, of course, some preschool children may resort to unkind behaviour and tactics due to a lack of understanding or because their parents have inadvertently subjected them to their own prejudices and opinions.

It can be very difficult to know when a child is being bullied unless they actually tell you, and it is, therefore, very important that childminders and parents are attentive to the changes in a child. Some children will try to cover up any signs of bullying for fear of making matters worse and even if you feel you have sufficient evidence, which points to the fact that a child is being bullied, it can still be very difficult to sort things out without the cooperation of the victim.

Although some victims of bullying can cope admirably and have the ability to shrug off name-calling, others may be affected deeply and become withdrawn or even suicidal.

It is important to remember that some children inadvertently set themselves up to be victims. Children who are shy and find it difficult to make friends, for example, are prime targets for bullies as they can be certain that these types of children are unlikely to stand up to them or fight back. Other, more outgoing popular children may also become victims of bullying, perhaps, because of an overpowering nature or through unintentional aggravation or goading. A popular, pretty girl who appears to have lots going for her can become the victim of a jealous bully simply because they appear confident and admired; a bully may decide to take it upon themselves to bring the popular person 'down a peg or two' by subjecting them to harassment. However, it is often less assertive children who are the targets of bullying.

Recognition of bullying

If a child confides in you that they are being bullied, it is essential that you act upon the revelation. Reassure the child that you believe what they are telling you and that you will do all you can to help them sort the problem out. No matter how inconsequential the bullying may appear to you, remember name-calling can be just as traumatic to a child as a physical attack; never dismiss the allegation or encourage the child to either 'keep away from their attacker' or 'stand up to them and fight'. Although parents often offer this kind of advice, particularly to sons, as they do not wish their children to appear weak or victimized, the simple truth of the matter is that this kind of advice, no matter how well meaning, will be of no benefit to the child and faced with this kind of advice it is highly likely the child will continue to be bullied and worse still will probably end up hiding the fact. It is highly unlikely that a child who has made a plea for help and has been ignored, will do so for a second time.

Bullying can take on many forms including

- cruel text or e-mail messages
- damage to property
- ignoring someone
- intimidation
- name-calling
- racial insults
- rumour mongering
- sarcasm
- teasing

- theft of possessions
- threatening behaviour

Bullied children will often feel fearful, apprehensive, worthless, undermined and upset.

Of course, not all children will openly admit that they are being bullied and you will need to be attentive to any changes in a child or young person if you are to help them overcome this kind of behaviour. Childminders will get to know the children in their care very well over time and, unlike nursery settings, they will usually be in the advantageous position of having sole care of the children and should, therefore, find it easier to spot changes in behaviour or worrying signs which may point to the possibility of the child being bullied.

Some of the possible signs of bullying may include the following:

- **Attempting self-harm.**
- **Becoming withdrawn.**
- **Bedwetting.**
- **Being physically sick** – this could be the result of worry or may be self-inflicted to avoid having to go to school.
- **Complaints of illness such as tummy ache and headache** – children often feign illness to avoid having to go to school, or to avoid clubs or classes, if they are being bullied there.
- **Deterioration of school work** – if the child is usually hard working and does well in class but suddenly starts to lose interest and their school work is suffering you should be concerned.
- **Frequently 'losing' possessions** – this could be a sign of having had their possessions stolen by the bully.
- **Often appearing hungry** – this could be a sign of having their lunch or lunch money stolen from them by the bully.
- **Regression** – thumb sucking, rocking, comfort behaviour etc. is often a sign of uncertainty in a child who does not usually resort to this type of behaviour.
- **Regularly asking for or stealing money** – this may be coerced from them by the bully often to avoid recrimination.
- **Ripped clothing** – this could be a sign that the child has been involved in a fight or has been roughly handled by others.
- **Showing aggressive behaviour, which is otherwise out of character for the child.**
- **Suffering from troubled sleep or nightmares.**
- **Unexplained injuries** – these could be a sign of physical harm either by a bully or self-inflicted. You should be concerned if the child suddenly appears to be suffering from a lot of injuries which they cannot offer a satisfactory explanation for.

Understanding bullying

Bullying is a type of aggressive behaviour often associated with inadequacy and a need for domination. Bullies like to be in control and wield authority over their victims.

Often bullies feel unwanted or uncared for. Problems at home, such as divorce, or pressure from friends, can result in a child showing bullying tendencies.

If you discover that your child or a child whom you are caring for is inflicting distress on another child through bullying you must act to sort the problem out and put an end to the victim's suffering. It is important that you do not judge the child; however, you need to make it clear to them that their behaviour is unacceptable and that what they are doing is hurtful, wrong and is, ultimately, causing another individual distress and harm. There are a number of things you can do to try to sort the problem out:

- Talk to the child who is doing the bullying and try to get to the heart of why they feel it is necessary to behave in this way. Find out what is bothering them or triggering their behaviour.
- Make sure that they understand that it is their *behaviour* you do not like rather than themselves.
- Reassure the child that you are willing to help them and that you will work with them to find a way to change their unacceptable behaviour.
- Encourage the bully to make amends with their victim. Talk about how they can apologize for the suffering they have inflicted on the other person and explain why it is necessary to do so.
- Offer the child lots of praise and encouragement and ensure you acknowledge when they have behaved well and managed to control their temper or feelings.
- Be prepared to challenge a bully who retaliates or makes excuses for their behaviour such as 'it's only a joke' or 'he's taken it all the wrong way'. Be prepared to explain that jokes do not result in distress and harassment and make it clear that bullying is not funny and is never seen as harmless fun.

Helping and supporting bullies and their victims

In addition to helping and understanding the behaviour of the bully you can do a lot to help victims protect themselves against bullying. Some of these strategies involve the following:

- Reassuring the child that you love them and that you are on their side 100 per cent. Never dismiss the child's worries and make sure that *all* forms of bullying are treated seriously. Name-calling can be just as devastating to a child as actual physical attacks and both can be extremely traumatic.
- Find out if there are any 'triggers' which appear to have started the attacks of bullying. Sometimes a child can unintentionally goad or aggravate their attacker and it is necessary to establish whether the child is unwittingly making themselves a target for the bully.
- It may be that the child is quiet and shy and, therefore, finds it hard to make friends. If this is the case help them to build on their confidence and show them strategies for making friends. Encourage them to join clubs outside of school hours.
- Encourage the child to be more assertive. This should not be mistaken for being aggressive. Children do not need to fight to be assertive; they simply need to recognize that they do not have to put up with being mistreated and they should recognize that they have the right to be treated with respect.
- Reassure the child that they are not to blame for the bullying they are experiencing. Quite often both the bully and the victim will experience similar emotions of self-doubt and worthlessness.

- Try to discourage the child from crying in front of the bully or responding dramatically to their threats and behaviour as this can quite often encourage their behaviour and lead to more bullying. Bullies enjoy seeing their victims become distressed and upset and this is the kind of response they are looking for. Insist that the child walks away and, if possible, get them to tell an adult immediately.
- Work out with the child ways of minimizing the opportunities for the bullying to take place. Encourage the child to spend as much time as possible around other people and to avoid spending lots of time alone.
- Encourage the child to be prepared for the bully's taunts. Quite often a child who has a planned response will feel more in control of the situation and begin to feel more assertive.
- Encourage the child to confide in a favourite teacher, someone they can talk to and feel confident about.
- Offer lots of love, praise and encouragement. A child who is being bullied will be stripped of their self-esteem and may feel useless and even deserving of the suffering they are receiving.
- It is important that adults think carefully before taking any action. Thoughtless action can be just as damaging as taking no action at all and children need to know that the adults they confide in will see things from their perspective and understand the situation they are in.
- Wherever possible, work out a strategy *with* the child for dealing with the bullying. Do not take sudden action.

Childminders must inform the parents of a child who has confided in them that they are being bullied even if the child has asked them not to. Never promise to keep the information a secret; if you are to help the child overcome the bullying problems then you will need to speak to their parents and possibly even their teachers, although no action should be taken without first discussing it with the child.

Exercise

Think of a way you can introduce the subject of bullying to your setting and hopefully encourage children to talk about their feelings and experiences.

Both bullies and their victims can benefit from learning basic self-assertive skills. Self-assertiveness can help a child to feel good about themselves and gives them a sense of well-being.

It must be understood that assertiveness is *not* the same as aggression. Most people will fall into one of three following categories:

- **Passive** – These people are of the opinion that other people's rights matter more than their own. They usually lack self-esteem and confidence. Victims are often passive people.
- **Assertive** – These people respect both themselves and others equally. This is how we should strive to be.

- **Aggressive** – These people behave as if their rights are more important than the rights of others. Bullies are often aggressive people.

For a child to practice being assertive you will need to encourage them to do the following:

- Avoid arguments.
- Avoid getting angry and upset.
- Be prepared for all eventualities – plan ahead and prepare their response.
- Don't make excuses – offer alternatives.
- Know their own mind and be clear about what they want.
- Learn how to say 'no' and mean it. If they are not happy with a certain situation they should not be pressured into giving in but should learn to stand firm.
- Learn how to 'blank' the taunts. Responding to insults with insults can end up making matters unbearable. Either ignore the insults and walk away or reply with a simple 'that's your opinion' or 'maybe' and then walk away. If the bully doesn't get the response they are looking for, it is quite likely they will become bored and give up. Bullies often feel a failure if they do not excite any kind of response from their victims and rather than looking foolish in front of their friends they often tend to back down.

Managing Children's Behaviour

How a child's behaviour can affect the safety of the setting

It is crucial that children are made aware that how they behave can have an enormous impact on everyone in the setting and that they understand the importance of abiding by the rules set to ensure the safety of everyone present. Childminders have a duty to the children in their care to ensure their safety at all times and, in order for them to do this effectively, they need to follow suitable strategies for dealing with behaviour. Unruly children who run around indoors, jumping on furniture and who have no regard for others are putting everyone in danger, and it is vital that a childminder takes control of the situation and responds to such behaviour in a constructive way.

Disruptive behaviour is not only dangerous in a childminding setting it is also unwelcome and can make the other children present feel resentful and uncomfortable. Children need to be active in their learning and it is the duty of the childminder to provide activities and opportunities that will stimulate and engage the children in their care. A lack of stimulation can often lead to boredom, which will result in attention seeking or disruptive behaviour. There is also the added danger that a child who is not adequately stimulated may become withdrawn and lose the ability to concentrate having wandered off into a world of their own to escape the tedium of their surroundings.

Managing children's behaviour

Childminders have a responsibility to manage and respond to children's behaviour and they should be confident in the way that they do this. It is very important that childminders work with the child's parents to ensure that there is continuity of behaviour management and that everyone understands the policies and procedures of the setting.

It can sometimes be difficult for childminders working with children from several families to ensure that everyone's wishes are taken into account, and it may, at times, be necessary for them to explain the reasoning behind their policies for everyone to feel welcome and valued.

The key to managing a child's behaviour effectively is good supervision. Most children will resort to inappropriate behaviour either because they are bored and lacking stimulation or because there are no adults present and they feel they can 'get away with it'. Both these causes are a direct result of the childminder's inability to address certain issues. It is the childminder's job to make sure that the activities and experiences provided are age-appropriate and that they offer suitable stimulation and children should always be supervised adequately. This, however, is not to say that squabbles, tantrums and fall-outs will not still occur from time to time and child care practitioners need to know how to respond to such behaviour.

Giving children choices helps them to learn that, while there may be several options available, they can only choose one at a time and this will enable them to realize the importance of sharing and taking turns. Allowing children the freedom of choice will encourage them to make the right decisions and enable them to learn that some things can be achieved immediately while others may take longer. Children who receive warm, responsive care are more likely to feel secure and valued and, subsequently, will learn to differentiate right from wrong which is, ultimately, what we are striving to achieve with any kind of behaviour management. Essentially, adults should be trying to get children to behave well because they *want* to rather than because they *have* to!

There are certain 'signs' that a childminder should be aware of which may indicate that children are becoming bored and may resort to inappropriate behaviour and these include the following:

- Petting squabbling and bickering.
- Heated arguments.
- Raised voices.
- Silence.
- Toys and equipment being used inappropriately or being thrown carelessly around the room.

Often the behaviour a child exhibits will reflect the way they are feeling about themselves or it may be a direct response to what is happening in their lives. For example, a child who is experiencing problems at home may become destructive or demanding whereas a child whose birthday is approaching may become over excited and impatient.

In general, behaviour falls into the following categories and these are

- attention seeking behaviour
- comfort behaviour
- destructive behaviour
- inappropriate verbal behaviour
- submissive behaviour

Attention seeking behaviour

Children exhibiting this kind of behaviour may be clingy, rude, demanding or challenging. This kind of behaviour is often associated with children who are insecure and who may have difficulty socializing with peers. Some children, who may not receive adequate attention at home, may resort to attention seeking behaviour as a way of being 'looked at' and often this type of behaviour is a sign of insecurity and low self-esteem. Adults should try to ignore this kind of behaviour, as much as possible, while making sure that the child receives lots of praise when they show appropriate behaviour.

Comfort behaviour

Children exhibiting this kind of behaviour may rock, suck their thumb, twiddle their hair or masturbate. This kind of behaviour is usually associated with children who are tired or bored, who have feelings of fear or anxiety or who may have serious emotional problems. It is important that childminders realize that masturbation is common in very young children, particularly boys. Adults should try to distract children showing this kind of behaviour or consider the possibility that the child may need to rest or could be feeling under the weather.

Destructive behaviour

Children exhibiting this kind of behaviour may throw objects or toys, resort to temper tantrums, lash out by biting or kicking, break or damage property. This type of behaviour is usually associated with children who are frustrated perhaps through a developmental delay, for example, or who may be suffering from serious emotional problems. Adults should remain as calm as possible when dealing with destructive behaviour and talk quietly to the child to try to get to the root of the problem. If the child poses a danger to themselves or others they should be removed from the situation until they have had the chance to calm down.

Inappropriate verbal behaviour

Children exhibiting this kind of behaviour may swear, speak inappropriately about matters of a sexual nature, offer racist remarks, taunt or tease others. This type of behaviour is often associated with insecure children or those not old enough to fully understand what they are saying. Often children will overhear adult remarks about something inappropriate and, having not completely understood what has been said, they may repeat the phrase without actually realizing that it is offensive. Older children who resort to this kind of behaviour will obviously understand what they are saying is inappropriate and children with low self-esteem may see this behaviour as a way of promoting their self-importance and making themselves appear more grown-up among their peers. Adults should challenge this kind of behaviour by asking the child where they have heard the phrase and what understanding they have of it. Older children should be told that their behaviour is unacceptable and hurtful.

Submissive behaviour

Children exhibiting this kind of behaviour will be withdrawn, fearful and anxious. They may be prone to being bullied. This type of behaviour is often associated with children who lack confidence and social skills. Adults should encourage the child to be more assertive and offer lots of praise and encouragement for their achievements.

In the majority of cases a child's own family will set the ground rules for what is and is not considered acceptable behaviour and, on the whole, children need to learn how to behave in a socially acceptable manner if they are to grow up to become respected members of the community. Behaviour management is a gradual process whereby most children will, at some point, test the boundaries, to see what they can and cannot get away with.

Many adults are quick to label a child as being 'naughty', 'disruptive' or 'uncooperative' without actually looking at the reasons behind their behaviour. Childminders need to look at the child as a 'whole' and understand why they may be behaving in a certain way before they can begin to manage the child's behaviour effectively.

There are certain factors in a child's life which will affect the way they behave and these may include

- age
- bereavement
- birth of a sibling
- child abuse
- gender
- moving house
- race, culture and religion
- re-marriage
- separation and divorce

A child's unwanted behaviour usually falls into two categories and these are

- short-term unwanted behaviour
- long-term unwanted behaviour

Short-term unwanted behaviour

This is usually the result of an occurrence which may have a negative impact on the child for a short period of time such as feeling tired or unwell or it may be due to circumstances which need adjusting to such as moving house or school, excitement due to an approaching birthday or other celebration.

Long-term unwanted behaviour

This is usually the result of more serious factors such as the child suffering from abuse, being taken into care or the death of a parent, and the behaviour the child is showing is likely to go on for some time.

It is very important that adults promote positive behaviour in children so that they understand and accept what is expected of them. Positive behaviour can be promoted in several ways

- Helping children understand how to behave appropriately and why.
- Praising good behaviour.
- Setting clear and consistent boundaries which are fair and appropriate to the age and understanding of the child they are aimed at.
- Developing self-esteem.
- Using rewards.
- Allowing children the opportunity to express themselves and to be in control of situations.

Using rewards to show you are pleased with a child's behaviour should not be mistaken with bribing the child. Childminders need to think carefully about the kind of rewards they intend to use and make sure that these are appropriate to the kind of behaviour shown. For example, a large bag of sweets to reward a child who has put their hand to their mouth when they have sneezed would be completely inappropriate whereas verbal recognition of the polite way the child dealt with the sneeze would be fine. You need to make sure that you do not over-indulge children and inundate them with rewards as you will risk getting them to behave in a certain way simply for the reward on offer rather than because they accept that this is appropriate. Rewards do not have to be sweets and, indeed, in many cases offering sweets would be inappropriate and may even go against the wishes of the child's parents. Other rewards you may consider using are stickers, verbal recognition and praise, star charts or being allowed to choose the next story or activity (see Figure 7.1).

Responding to unwanted behaviour

It is important to remember that children cannot behave impeccably all the time and, indeed, adults should not expect them to do so. Testing the boundaries and pushing limits are all part of growing up and children need to be able to express themselves and find their feet. There are, of course, certain things that childminders can do to effectively eliminate some of the

Figure 7.1 Reward charts can be a good way of recognizing a child's good behaviour.
Source: Lee, A., (2008)

factors which may cause children to behave inappropriately and you should consider how the child feels before deciding on a suitable sanction. For example, the child may be showing unwanted behaviour because they are

- tired
- bored
- anxious
- frustrated
- restricted
- unwell

Most of these reasons can be dealt with easily and, if you are doing your job correctly, it is probably true to say that the majority of these situations should never arise in the first place! It is worth remembering that children may also show signs of unacceptable behaviour if they are unsure of what is expected of them or if they do not have clear, consistent boundaries to follow.

Children, particularly those of a young age, often have difficulty controlling their emotions and feelings and, as a result, they may become angry, frustrated or weepy for no apparent reason. Childcare practitioners should encourage the child to explore their emotions and talk about how they are feeling. Children need to know that, although sometimes very powerful, emotions should not be feared and they need to understand that everyone experiences emotions. Children can be very sensitive and will often feel angry or frustrated if they consider that they are being unfairly treated or left out. Take the time to explain your rules and make sure that everyone understands the importance of taking turns and being considerate. Explain to the children what your rules are in a way appropriate to their age and understanding and help them to understand why these rules exist.

In order for everyone in the childcare setting to feel welcome, valued and secure, you will need to have a set of boundaries for everyone to follow. All children need boundaries. Boundaries put a limit on behaviour and enable a child to understand what is and is not acceptable. Boundaries help a child to feel safe and secure. When thinking about the kind of boundaries to set you will need to consider

- the number of children you are caring for;
- the ages of the children you are caring for;
- the level of understanding of the children you are caring for.

Your boundaries need to be fair and realistic and they need to be acceptable to the parents of the children you provide care for.

It is important when setting your boundaries that you stick to your decision. There is little point in creating a framework for managing children's behaviour if you back down at the first sign of a problem. When you say 'no' to a child you must mean it. By using the word sparingly you will hopefully manage to get the children to realize that this word is final. 'No' should not give the impression that you are doubtful or open to persuasion. If a child thinks they can sway your decision by throwing a tantrum you are asking for trouble.

When dealing with unwanted behaviour it is important to

- remain calm at all times;
- use methods of distraction if necessary;
- warn the child of any consequences they may encounter if they persist in showing unwanted behaviour;
- make a fresh start after the incident and refrain from referring to the behaviour again.

Childminders should never

- use any form of physical punishment to deal with unwanted behaviour this includes, smacking, shaking, pinching, shoving or rough handling of any kind;
- shouting;
- criticism;
- humiliation;
- isolation.

When dealing with an incident of unwanted behaviour you should follow this procedure:

- **Tell the child 'no'** – most children will respond to a firm 'no'. This works particularly well if used with eye contact and verbal expressions. The tone of voice used is also very important.

- **Explain to the child what will happen if their unacceptable behaviour persists** – children should always be made aware of the consequences of their actions as this underlines the importance of the rules and reiterates the boundaries.
- **Carry out the sanction** – if you threaten to carry out a particular sanction, should the child persist in showing unacceptable behaviour, it is paramount that you see your threat through. Idle threats will undermine your authority and confuse the child. Removal of a toy or equipment should be the last resort, but if compromises and warnings have been ineffective, then you will need to remove the toy or equipment until such a time as the child has rectified their behaviour.
- **Time out** – time out should never be mistaken for isolation. Children should never be placed in isolation this is not an effective form of behaviour management. A few minutes of time out whereby a child is removed from the situation which is causing them a problem should be sufficient for them to calm down and address their behaviour. This method of behaviour management is more suited to older children. Time out should not be seen as a punishment. It is a means of getting the child to calm down and reflect on the way they are behaving.

Other effective methods of dealing with unwanted behaviour include ignoring the behaviour, distracting the child or providing play therapy, all of which can be beneficial.

Ignoring the behaviour – often children who resort to unwanted behaviour do so to seek attention. By giving the child your attention when they are behaving badly you are effectively 'rewarding' them. Some children will see any attention favourably and even if the attention they are gaining is through unacceptable behaviour they will see this as better than no attention at all. Try to busy yourself with something else and do not respond to the child. A child who is behaving badly but not having the desired effect in that you are not reacting to them will quickly tire of the situation. Always make sure that any behaviour, which poses a danger to the child or someone else is not ignored and in cases such as these you may like to try using:

Distraction – sometimes children will cause a scene or throw a tantrum when they cannot get their own way. Little things which may seem inconsequential to the adults around them, may be blown out of all proportion and, to prevent this kind of eruption occurring, distraction can be very effective. For example, if a child decides they want a toy someone else is playing with and can clearly not have it then, instead of simply denying them what they want, try offering another toy in its place.

Play therapy – this can be a very effective way of helping children to cope with stress and anxiety and it is a good way of releasing strong emotions in a safe, non-threatening environment. For example, play therapy can be used for a child who is feeling frustrated by offering them a ball to kick outside or clay to knead. An anxious child who may be fearful of going into hospital or starting a new school can be encouraged to act out their emotions through role play.

Writing and implementing behaviour policies

It is important, when caring for children from different families, to ensure that you are flexible in your approach to behaviour management in order to take into account the views and wishes of the parents of the children. However, you must also ensure that you are consistent so that children do not become confused. Talk your policies through with the parents and children and, if necessary, adapt them to take everyone's preferences into account. Issue parents with a copy of your policies and, if necessary, get them to sign to say that they agree to them. You may need to refer to the policy at a later date should any problems arise.

Boundaries in the childminding setting need to be consistent with those at home for children to be confident in understanding what is and is not acceptable. Having different rules for them to follow at different times is not a good idea.

It is always a good idea to take a positive approach rather than being negative about children's behaviour and try, whenever possible, to offer suggestions rather than orders. For example, children will respond better to a suggestion to 'play with the ball outside' rather than to a demand to 'stop playing with the ball indoors'. The child, who wants to play with the ball has been offered the chance to do what he likes but outside instead of indoors; however, he has not been stopped from playing with the ball. The outcome here would be very different to the child being told to simply stop playing with the ball.

Exercise

Think of positive ways you can use in response to a child who is
- running indoors.
- teasing the dog.
- spoiling the picture their brother is painting.

Before beginning to write a policy for promoting good behaviour in your childminding setting you first need to ask yourself a number of questions:

- What will I accept?
- What kind of behaviour will I not tolerate?
- Why do I think my boundaries are necessary?
- Can the children in my care be expected to understand the boundaries I have set?
- Are the boundaries fair?
- How do the children's parents feel about the boundaries I have set?

There is little point in producing a list of things you expect the children in your care to abide by if these are inappropriate or unnecessary. For your behaviour policy to be effective it needs to be short, relevant and easy to implement. If you have points on your policy which are not relevant to the children you are currently caring for then remove them.

Think about how you would like to see children behave in your setting. Positive behaviour should involve

- sharing and taking turns
- being cooperative
- being kind and considerate
- being helpful
- being polite
- taking responsibility

Unacceptable behaviour includes

- being rude
- being mean
- being uncooperative
- refusing to tidy up
- refusing to share and take turns
- throwing tantrums
- being destructive
- climbing on furniture
- being noisy – screaming and shouting
- taking food without asking permission

There are many ways you can show your appreciation of a child's behaviour and you should decide which of these are suitable to certain tasks and which are appropriate to children depending on their age and level of development; for example, you could encourage positive behaviour by

- smiling;
- commenting positively about the child's behaviour;
- saying 'thank you';
- giving the child a sticker or adding a token to your behaviour chart;
- mentioning the child's positive behaviour to their parents;
- giving the child the chance to choose the next activity;
- giving the child more responsibility as a result of their positive achievement.

Exercise

Write your own behaviour policy to be used in your childminding setting taking into account everything we have covered in this chapter. Make sure that your policy is short and easy for the children to understand and implement.

Protecting the Childcare Practitioner

As childminders usually work alone they and their families can be particularly vulnerable to allegations made against them. It is absolutely vital, therefore, that any incidents which take place during the course of your childminding day are appropriately recorded and that parents are informed about them and requested to sign in agreement of the explanation you have given.

Why childminders are vulnerable against allegations

Thankfully, serious allegations against childminders appear to be far and few between; however, it is worth practicing safe methods which will, hopefully, deter individuals from making allegations against you. Occasionally, some parents may accuse their child's carer of misconduct to cover up their own guilt or negligence. On other occasions parents may jump to the wrong conclusions or believe malicious gossip/rumours, which may bring about cause for their concern. Childminders can and should take some very simple steps to avoid allegations being made against them. These steps include the following:

- Recording, in writing, any accidents or incidents which may have happened to a child in your care. Follow-up your written account by explaining clearly and concisely what has occurred to the parent and requesting that they sign your record to show their acknowledgement and acceptance of your explanation.
- If a child arrives at your house with an obvious injury, record this injury, and if necessary make a quick sketch of the injury; ask the parent to explain how the injury occurred, record this

explanation and ensure that the parent signs your record so that you can prove, if necessary at a later date, that the child sustained the injury away from your setting.

- The teenage sons of childminders are particularly vulnerable to allegations of abuse. Never leave young children alone with your teenagers to avoid this kind of allegation.
- Make sure that you maintain confidentiality at all times.
- Make sure that you report any suspicions you may have of abuse, neglect or mistreatment of a child to your Local Safeguarding Children Board, social services or the NSPCC.
- If you are concerned about the way a child in your care is playing, speaking or behaving, inform the parent of your concerns.
- Make sure that you always conduct your own behaviour in a professional manner and that you use appropriate language when caring for children.
- Take your lead from the child. Never ask for cuddles, always take your cue from the child. Not all children are openly affectionate and if they are reluctant to respond in this way never put pressure on them.
- Never leave children unattended.
- Never leave children in the care of someone who is unauthorized.
- Avoid any kind of rough handling whether this is in the form of play fighting or when dealing with unwanted behaviour.
- Encourage children to become independent as soon as possible, particularly in areas of carrying out personal tasks, such as wiping their own bottoms after visiting the toilet.
- Always speak to the children kindly and with respect.
- Be honest and open with the children.
- Never ask a child to keep a secret no matter how innocent it may be.
- Be approachable and make sure that the children can talk to you about things which may concern them but never prompt them to open up to you if they clearly do not wish to.
- Teach children how to protect themselves.
- Keep up-to-date with training and attend classes about child protection.

Childminders are in positions of trust and as such you must act responsibly at all times. It is an unfortunate part of a childcare practitioner's job that sometimes we may be vulnerable to allegations of mistreating a child or accusations of abuse. Childminders and nannies may even be more vulnerable than other childcare practitioners as they usually work alone and, therefore, do not have the support or backup of colleagues working with them.

Your records can be vital in protecting yourself against allegations of misconduct or abuse, particularly, if you have reported a case of child abuse, as the guilty party may be intent on looking to put the blame on someone else (see Figure 8.1).

How to protect yourself and your family from allegations

One of the best ways of protecting yourself and your family from allegations is to take a professional approach at all times and maintain confidentiality. Respecting confidentiality can, at times, be hard, and sometimes childminders may breach a confidence without even

Figure 8.1 Childminders can be particularly vulnerable to allegations. Always record any incidents or accidents clearly and date them.
Source: Lee, A. (2008)

knowing they have done so. It is important to think before you speak and to remember that, as a childminder, you may be privy to information of a sensitive nature. If a parent tells you something in confidence it is very important that you do not break this confidence by gossiping to others. The only time you should break the rule of confidentiality is when it is in the interests of the child to do so, for example, if you need to seek professional advice in the case of a child protection issue and even then you should only discuss a child's details with those who need to know. Idle gossip is never acceptable.

Sometimes childminders can be put in the unfortunate position of being questioned by a parent about another child in their care or their family and it can be difficult for childminders to know what to do in these circumstances. Although it is important not to be rude you should not divulge sensitive information through gossip just to appease someone. Think how you would feel if the person being talked about were you!

Exercise

Spend a little time thinking about what kinds of things parents in your setting usually talk about. Are some parents more prone to asking questions about children in your care and their families? Do they ask things of a sensitive nature or are they simply passing the time of day?

There may be times when people make comments in passing about certain things and you should use your professional judgement when determining whether these occasions are breaching confidentiality. Generally speaking, discussing every day things like holiday destinations, disclosing the age of a child or discussing things that certain children like or dislike is not usually seen as breaching confidentiality or speaking out-of-turn; however, you should never divulge information about important issues such as

- a child's medical information
- parents' relationship problems
- court orders concerning a child's residence or contacts with family members
- family set-ups
- suspicions of child abuse
- developmental issues about the child.

Think about the times when you are more at risk of unintentionally talking out-of-turn such as in the playground or at support meetings and try to be ready with a response if you feel someone is asking you something you are unhappy answering. Instead of refusing point blank to speak to someone try saying something along the lines of 'I don't know about that' or 'the parents don't divulge information of that nature to me'. This should put an end to most people's questionings; however, if someone is particularly persistent in trying to glean information, always be professional and, if necessary, explain your duty to the child in your care and their family and explain that you are not prepared to discuss confidential matters with them.

If you are in any doubt about what is and is not acceptable to disclose play it safe and say nothing!

It is vital, however, that in order to protect yourself and your family against allegations you must understand when you need to breach confidentiality and whom you should speak to. It is important that you are guided by the interests of the child when making your decision as to what to divulge and to who, but generally speaking, suspected cases of child abuse need to be discussed with other professionals as would your knowledge of a child's medical history if you have had to take the child to hospital following an accident and the parents are not immediately available.

Working in partnership with parents

It is paramount that childminders understand that parents are the most important people in their child's life. It is the duty of the childminder to work *with* the child's parents not *against* them and to acknowledge that they are the most knowledgeable people with regard to their child. You should never be trying to take the place of the child's parent and it is important that you do not try to compete with the parents for the child's affections. Listen to and respect the wishes of the parents at all times and make sure that you exchange information with them about their child on a daily basis.

Good childminding practice is based on respect for each other. Family values, lifestyles, beliefs and traditions should all be considered.

A childminder should never make a parent feel inadequate or uninformed; this is not always easy particularly in the case of new, inexperienced parents who are finding their feet when it comes to parenting issues. Offer support and advice, when asked for, and never criticize or judge parents. Parenting is a very complex role and no two families are alike. It is important to remember that there is no single, correct way to bring up children, and what works well for some families, may be totally unacceptable for others. Parents need to find what works for them and you need to support the decisions they make.

Sharing information on a daily basis with parents is essential not only for the welfare of the child, but also to ensure your own and your family's protection. Any suspicions you may have about a change in a child's behaviour, for example, should be recorded and discussed with the parents, provided you do not feel that the change in behaviour is due to some kind of abuse which, if discussed with the parent, may put the child in danger. Make sure that you are thorough with your explanations if you are worried about something and, if necessary arrange to meet the parent at a later time or telephone them when you have finished work so that you can discuss your concerns without the distractions of other children around you. Don't demand a response from the parent or lay down the law if the child has behaved inappropriately. Explain the situation calmly and decide *together* on a suitable strategy to deal with the situation. Agree on appropriate action and work as a team to get things back on track.

Always remember that families will at times come under stress, and as a result, they may find themselves struggling or being unable to cope. Once again, be there to support them if necessary. Never judge them or offer unwanted advice. Factors which cause stress may include

- separation or divorce
- redundancy
- bereavement
- birth of a new baby
- moving house
- major accidents
- disability

There is always the possibility, of course, that parents may not divulge information of a sensitive nature to you and, therefore, you will have no way of telling whether they are under any pressures or strains. It is, therefore, essential that you refrain from being judgemental of the way *any* parent chooses to bring up their child.

List of Useful Addresses and Websites

Aids helpline – 0800 567123

Alcoholics Anonymous – 0345 697555

Anti Bullying Campaign – 020 7378 1446 **www.bullying.co.uk (accessed 23 Feburary 2008)**

Barnardo's – 020 8550 8822 **www.barnardos.org.uk (accessed 23 Feburary 2008)**

Child Accident Prevention Trust (CAPT) – 020 7608 3828 **www.capt.org.uk (accessed 23 Feburary 2008)**

Childline – 0800 1111 **www.childline.co.uk (accessed 23 Feburary 2008)**

Department of Health – **www.doh.gov.uk (accessed 23 Feburary 2008)**

Department for Children, Schools and Families (DfES) – 0845 60 222 60 **www.teachernet.gov.uk/publica-tions or www.dfes.gov.uk (accessed 23 Feburary 2008)**

Drugs helpline – 0800 776600

Eating Disorders Association – 0845 634 7650 **www.edauk.com (accessed 23 Feburary 2008)**

Family Friends of Lesbian and Gays – 01454 852 418 **www.fflag.org.uk (accessed 23 Feburary 2008)**

Family Planning – 0845 310 1334 **www.fpa.org.uk (accessed 23 Feburary 2008)**

Family Rights Group – 0800 731 1696

Information for Teenagers about Sex and Relationships **www.ruthinking.co.uk (accessed 23 Feburary 2008)**

Internet Watch Hotline – 0845 600 8844

Kidscape – 08451 205 204 **www.kidscape.org.uk (accessed 23 Feburary 2008)**

Message Home – 0800 700 740

Missing Persons – 0500 700 700 **www.missingpersons.org (accessed 23 Feburary 2008)**

National Children's Bureau – 020 7843 6000 **www.ncb.org.uk (accessed 23 Feburary 2008)**

National Drugs Helpline (FRANK) – 0800 77 66 00 **www.talktofrank.com (accessed 23 Feburary 2008)**

NHS Direct – 0845 4647 **www.nhsdirect.nhs.uk (accessed 23 Feburary 2008)**

NSPCC – 0808 800 5000 **www.nspcc.org.uk (accessed 23 Feburary 2008)**

Parentline Plus – 020 7284 5500 **www.parentlineplus.org.uk (accessed 23 Feburary 2008)**

Relate – **www.relate.org.uk (accessed 23 Feburary 2008)**

Royal Society for the Prevention of Accidents (RoSPA) 0121 248 2000 **www.rospa.com (accessed 23 Feburary 2008)**

Samaritans – 0845 790 9090

Save the Children – 020 7703 5400 **www.savethechildren.org.uk (accessed 23 Feburary 2008)**

Shelter – 0800 446441

Smokers Quitline – 0800 002200

Victim Support – 01702 333 911

Bibliography

Child Accident Prevention Trust 2007, *Safer Children, Healthier Lives*, London: Child Accident Prevention Trust.

DfES Publications 2007, *Practice Guidance for the Early Years Foundation Stage*, Nottingham: DfES Publications.

DfES Publications 2005, *The National Standards for Under Eights Day Care and Childminding*, Nottingham: DfES Publications.

Lee, A. 2007a, *The Childminder's Companion*, Oxford: How to Books Ltd.

Lee, A. 2007b, *Childminder's Handbook*, London: Continuum International Publishing Group.

Index